DISCOVER CHOCOLATE

DISCOVER CHOCOLATE

The Ultimate Guide to
Buying, Tasting, and Enjoying
Fine Chocolates

CLAY GORDON

Publisher of Chocophile.com and founder
of the New World Chocolate Society

GOTHAM BOOKS

GOTHAM BOOKS
Published by Penguin Group (USA) Inc.
375 Hudson Street, New York, New York 10014, U.S.A.
Penguin Group (Canada), 90 Eglinton Avenue East, Suite 700, Toronto, Ontario M4P 2Y3, Canada (a division of Pearson Penguin
Canada Inc.); Penguin Books Ltd, 80 Strand, London WC2R 0RL, England; Penguin Ireland, 25 St Stephen's Green, Dublin 2,
Ireland (a division of Penguin Books Ltd); Penguin Group (Australia), 250 Camberwell Road, Camberwell, Victoria 3124, Australia
(a division of Pearson Australia Group Pty Ltd); Penguin Books India Pvt Ltd, 11 Community Centre, Panchsheel Park, New Delhi-
110 017, India; Penguin Group (NZ), 67 Apollo Drive, Rosedale, North Shore 0745, Auckland, New Zealand (a division of Pearson
New Zealand Ltd); Penguin Books (South Africa) (Pty) Ltd, 24 Sturdee Avenue, Rosebank, Johannesburg 2196, South Africa

Penguin Books Ltd, Registered Offices: 80 Strand, London WC2R 0RL, England

Published by Gotham Books, a division of Penguin Group (USA) Inc.

First printing, October 2007
10 9 8 7 6 5 4 3 2 1

Copyright © 2007 by Quirk Packaging, Inc.
Maps copyright © 2007 by Digital Cartographics
Photo credits appear on page 160.
All rights reserved

Gotham Books and the skyscraper logo are trademarks of Penguin Group (USA) Inc.

LIBRARY OF CONGRESS CATALOGING-IN-PUBLICATION DATA HAS BEEN APPLIED FOR.

ISBN 978-1-592-40308-0

A Quirk Packaging Book
Designed by Stislow Design + Illustration
Photo editing by Wendy Missan
Text editing by Liana Krissoff
Illustrations by John Stislow
Printed in China

While the author has made every effort to provide accurate telephone numbers and Internet addresses at the time of publication,
neither the publisher nor the author assumes any responsibility for errors, or for changes that occur after publication. Further, the
publisher does not have any control over and does not assume any responsibility for author or third-party websites or their content.

To my wife Adrienne and daughters Catherine, Diane, Erica, and Alexandra, without whom it would not have been possible for me to have the resources, the time, or the courage to follow my own path of chocolate discovery. To my parents and my sisters Amelia and Kate for always being there when I needed them, and to my extended family for their support, encouragement, and willingness to listen while I learned.

Alexandra in Paris at age six: Discovering the delights of chocolate fish.

✳

Contents

DISCOVER CHOCOLATE

Introduction

YOU, TOO, CAN BECOME A CHOCOLATE CRITIC

＊

When I tell people that I am a professional chocolate critic, the most common response is, "How did you get that job?" The truth is, I didn't so much get this job as make it. There are movie critics and theater critics and art critics and restaurant critics and wine critics—in fact, there are critics for pretty much everything you can think of. But back in 1994 when I wanted to start learning about chocolate, I couldn't find a single chocolate critic to guide me. So I set out to become one, and the book you're reading now is the summation (to date) of what I've learned that will be (I hope) interesting and useful to you as you delve deeper into the world of chocolate.

I got seriously interested in chocolate after a trip to Cannes, France, where I discovered a huge selection of chocolate bars at a gourmet store. (Are you one of those people who, minutes after setting foot in a new city, scopes out the nearest chocolate shop? Me, too.) I bought several interesting-looking bars to bring home and learned by translating the text on the wrappers that they were each made from beans that came from exotic-sounding places—Ceylon, Trinite, Equateur, Chuao, Puerto Cabello. Some locations were easy to decipher (Ceylon is Sri Lanka, Trinite is Trinidad, Equateur is Ecuador), but others mystified me. Where was Puerto Cabello? (It's in Venezuela, I soon learned.)

About a week after my return, I had a dinner party at my apartment where I held my first chocolate tasting. I broke the bars into pieces, tore the place names off the wrappers, and passed the plates around. What struck

Are you one of those people who scopes out the nearest chocolate shop minutes after setting foot in a new city?

me that night was not only that all of the chocolates tasted different, but that each of us at the tasting had a different favorite—and for different reasons. This experience led me to search for further information, but I quickly realized how little information about chocolate there was to be found. I came across lots of recipes that used chocolate but almost nothing on the subjects that interested me: Where does chocolate come from? How is it made? Where can I buy the best chocolate? How can I distinguish a great chocolate from a bad one? (Believe me, there is such a thing as bad chocolate.)

I began a quest to discover these answers. It took me almost seven years to get to the point where I was confident enough in what I knew to hang out my shingle as a professional chocolate critic, and in May 2001 I started publishing the website Chocophile.com. The site started out as a labor of love—no e-commerce, no advertising. It was a blog, a place to share my interest in chocolate with everyone else on the Internet. At about the same time I also started giving tasting classes, where I was learning just as much as the people I was supposed to be teaching.

Years later, I'm still learning new things about chocolate. I'd be lying if I said that eating the stuff all day long isn't the best thing about being a chocolate critic. But I've found that knowing where it grows, how it's made, who makes it, and putting together all the interesting little pieces in the larger puzzle that is each individual chocolate, helps me to truly taste it. Picking out certain distinctive characteristics, like a wine drinker noticing the signs of oak-barrel aging in a California Chardonnay (too much? just enough? more than in the last Chardonnay I tried?), makes comparisons among different chocolates more meaningful and my appreciation of them richer—and it'll boost your appreciation, too.

But no good critic is motivated purely by the desire to appreciate (or criticize), and no one likes the guy who's determined to foist his opinions of what's good and bad on others. I want to share my passion for chocolate—the thrill I feel when I learn something new about how it's made or discover a new chocolatier or even a new way to approach this endlessly fascinating subject—and that's where the idea for this book came from. This is the first book that focuses on the experience of tasting chocolate; the information about growing, manufacturing, and buying chocolate all help prepare you to do just that. The end result? Your appreciation of what goes into making chocolate will be enhanced, which in turn will increase your enjoyment of chocolate by leaps and bounds.

Discover Chocolate will help you enjoy the chocolates you already love even more (who knew that was possible?) and lead you to new and exciting favorites. It will also help you to explore the best ways to experience chocolate, whether you prefer to pair it with a fine Madeira or a tall glass of cold milk or enjoy it straight up. It's my goal to show you how to become the best chocolate critic you can be for the only audience that truly matters: you. And if you understand not only what chocolates you like, but what it is you like about them and why they taste the way they do, this information will lead you to discover other enticing chocolate varieties and brands to add to your list of personal favorites. Because there's nothing wrong with more chocolate.

THE BEST CHOCOLATE IN THE WORLD

After a tasting a couple of years ago I was approached by a man in the class who wanted to know if I had ever heard of a tiny chocolatier in a town not far from Genoa, Italy, because they made the best chocolate in the world. I confessed that I was not familiar with the name of the shop and was not aware of ever having tasted its wares. My student went on to tell me that he'd recently returned from his honeymoon; he and his new bride had stopped in this small town (on what was undoubtedly a picture-postcard-perfect day) and bought some chocolate, then proceeded to eat it sitting by the (no doubt ancient) fountain in the (quaint and picturesque) town square.

Chocolate makes what might have been an ordinary meal, or an ordinary day, memorable.

Of course it was the best chocolate in the world—for him. Chocolate is one of those foods that seems to intensify a situation. It makes what might have been an ordinary meal, or an ordinary day, memorable—to say nothing of extraordinary days like the one my student surely had in the small town near Genoa. In other words, the circumstances in which we enjoy a certain chocolate tend to color our evaluation of it. I've spent years teaching myself to objectively assess and describe the quality of every morsel of chocolate I taste, but I'm still subject to purely emotional responses on occasion. (And what fun would life be if we didn't respond emotionally to chocolate?)

Chocolate is different from most other gourmet foods, however, because our tastes in chocolate as adults are rooted very strongly in childhood memories. Unlike wine, beer, and coffee, which we tend to start consuming only after we reach our teenage years (at the earliest), chocolate is something that most of us start eating at a very young age. It is very likely that the chocolate you appreciate most as an adult bears at least some relation to the chocolate you ate on special occasions as a child—it may taste very much like chocolate bunnies or gelt, or it may be their polar opposite. Either way, that early-childhood chocolate serves as an emotional touchstone, the chocolate you will probably compare all other chocolates to—that is, until another touchstone experience comes along.

I grew up in lots of places, but mostly southern California. Each year for my mom's birthday we got her a box of See's Victoria English Toffee: butter toffee with a thin layer of chocolate and ground almonds on each side. Each year for my dad's birthday we got him a box of House of Bauer Bavarian Mint Meltaways. For a long time, these were my chocolate touchstones. I compared all chocolate-almond toffees against my memory of See's, and mint meltaways were always compared to Bauer's.

My touchstone experiences are different from yours—not better, just different. If you grew up in the Midwest, chances are that a Whitman's Sampler was the special-occasion chocolate in your house, and, if not, it might have been a box of Russell Stover. It might have been Fannie Farmer or a local hometown favorite such as Fowler's in Buffalo, New York, or Ganong's in the Maritimes in Canada or Chilmark Chocolates on Martha's Vineyard off the coast of Massachusetts. Exactly what it was doesn't matter at this point other than the fact that it serves as your taste benchmark.

These anecdotes underscore a simple fact: the best chocolate in the world is the one you like best. This book will help you enlarge your experience with chocolate, first helping you fine-tune your tasting and descriptive skills to determine what exactly you like about certain chocolates, then introducing you to the world of the cacao grower and everything that goes into making chocolate and bon bons. Knowing what you like, as well as how and where chocolate is grown and produced, will help you become a smart consumer of chocolate, able to home in on the very best chocolates at the best prices wherever your travels take you. Finally, this book offers advice on how best to enjoy that chocolate once you have it in hand, pairing it, if you choose, with wines and spirits.

HOW TO USE THIS BOOK

✻

In this book you'll discover:

1. How to taste (not just eat) chocolate;
2. What you like in a chocolate;
3. Where cocoa beans are grown;
4. How chocolate is made;
5. The differences between good chocolate and great chocolate;
6. How and where to buy great chocolate;
7. Great beverage pairings for chocolate; and
8. Lots of other really interesting things about—you guessed it—chocolate!

The emphasis here is on learning to taste with a purpose: finding out what you like about chocolates and how to choose the best ones for you. The extensive coverage of cacao growing and the chocolate-making process is provided with the goal of increasing your awareness of where what you eat comes from and what went into producing it, much as information about where grapes were grown and how they were processed helps enhance a wine lover's appreciation. What you won't find here is a complete history of cacao—other books, several of them listed in the Resources section in the Appendix starting on page 154, together do an excellent job of recounting that fascinating tale, and I'd encourage you to expand on your knowledge of chocolate by reading them. Since chocolate has its own specific vocabulary, developed over time to reflect the unique aspects of the subject, a Glossary on page 145 provides definitions of the terms you need to know. Some of the words and their uses have been borrowed from the lexicon of other foods and beverages—wine in particular—and some are specific to chocolate.

What you won't find in this book are specific ratings and reviews of chocolate and other information that is likely to become out of date by the time you can buy this book. Please visit this book's companion website, DiscoverChocolate.com. Any updates to the information in this book will appear there. It's an invaluable resource of reviews of hundreds of great (and not so great) chocolates, and sources for popular, readily available chocolates along with rare, hard-to-find varieties. Consider the website an extension of the book that I hope will inspire you as you continue to make your own personal chocolate discoveries.

Enjoy!

Clay Gordon, Larchmont, NY
clay@discoverchocolate.com

I.

How to Taste Chocolate

A DELECTABLE METHOD TO INCREASE YOUR ENJOYMENT OF EVERY BITE

YOU PROBABLY ALREADY KNOW HOW TO EAT CHOCOLATE. ✳ And if you're reading this book, you probably already derive a lot of pleasure from the act. In fact, if you're the full-fledged chocophile I think you are, it might not be an exaggeration to say that you live for chocolate. (I know I do.) That said, it's very likely that you've only scratched the surface of the whole great, glorious chocolate experience, because you may have only *eaten* chocolate. If you've yet to *taste* chocolate, you're in for a real treat.

> ### "Nine of every ten persons say they love chocolate. The tenth lies."
> —Jean Anthelme Brillat-Savarin

The difference between *tasting* chocolate and *eating* chocolate is that tasting chocolate is a conscious and deliberate process, one in which you pay attention to every aspect of what you are eating and consciously evaluate the sensations you are experiencing. You don't have to *taste* every bite of chocolate you eat from now on, but when you come across a new chocolate that seems like it might deserve closer attention, ask yourself the questions on the opposite page. Your answers will help you identify what you like (or don't like) about it.

CHOCOPHILE FACT

Most adults (even in the U.S.) now say they prefer dark chocolate to milk chocolate.

＊

As with many fine foods and beverages, the more you know about what you're tasting the greater your ability to appreciate the subtleties that make each taste unique and interesting. In the following pages, you'll learn to identify exactly what it is you like about the chocolate you like and to keep track of what you've tasted and what you thought of it in a tasting journal. The point is certainly not to turn you into a chocolate snob, capable of eating only chocolate made from the rarest of ancient Criollo beans and then only if the cocoa content is above 69 percent. The point of learning to taste chocolate is to develop your tasting apparatus so that you can appreciate distinct features of a variety of chocolates and learn to pick out the ones that will give you the most pleasure in any given situation.

Once you have a better understanding of what you like about the chocolate you taste, in the next chapter you'll be taken deep inside the craft of chocolate making. Discovering where chocolate comes from, learning how the cocoa beans are grown and made into bars of chocolate, and then how that chocolate might be transformed into, say, a Champagne-infused truffle will enhance your understanding of chocolate—and ultimately your enjoyment.

* How is the chocolate presented?

* What does the chocolate look like?

* What does the chocolate feel and sound like when it is "snapped"?

* What does the chocolate smell like?

* What does the chocolate taste like?

* How does the chocolate feel on the tongue and how does it melt? What other physical sensations does the chocolate cause in your mouth?

* What memories does the chocolate evoke?

The most important attributes to bring to tasting chocolate are:

1. Focus and attention;
2. A clean, rested palate; and
3. Your sense of humor.

I have discovered that you don't have to be a supertaster to become a proficient chocolate taster (you just won't get a job tasting for Callebaut). You don't have to have a perfect taste memory, either, as long as you take good notes. All you really have to do is pay close attention to what you're eating. (And how hard can that be? It's *chocolate*.) As long as you are confident enough to bring your own senses and sensibilities to the tasting, and don't take yourself too seriously (chocolate promises pleasure for everyone, so don't get geeky or exclusive about it), you'll get a great deal out of any chocolate tasting. Repeat after me:

"It's just chocolate."

Are You a Supertaster?

Supertasters have more taste buds than "normal" tasters do. Not better taste buds, just more of them. To tell if you are supertaster, you'll need some blue food dye, a magnifying glass, a piece of paper with a hole that has a diameter of ¼ inch (6.4 millimeters), and a good friend. Place a drop of the blue food dye on your tongue and then cover the blue area with the paper so you can see the area that has been dyed blue through the hole. Get your friend to use the magnifying glass to count the number of pink spots—your taste buds— that can be seen. Opinions differ regarding the specifics, but in general, having more than thirty-five taste buds per ¼ inch (6.4 millimeters) means that you are a supertaster. Having fifteen to twenty taste buds means that you are a normal taster, and having fewer than fifteen taste buds means that you taste foods (including chocolate) mostly with your sense of smell.

SETTING THE STAGE

✳

For your first "serious" chocolate-tasting adventure, pick up a wide selection of bar (plain) chocolates, preferably all dark or all milk chocolates, from different makers and with different percentages of cocoa (80 percent, 70 percent, 68 percent, and so on). It's not important at this point to know exactly where the chocolates come from or whether they'll be complementary. It's not even important that you know how to read a chocolate label. (We'll get into chocolate buying in Chapter 3, which will show you how to become an ace chocolate consumer.) Each taster will need ¼ to ½ ounce (7 to 14 grams) of each chocolate for each level of the tasting pyramid, described in detail under Rating Your Chocolate, pages 44–47. For example, if you're going to taste eight chocolates, you'll need 1 to 2 ounces (28 to 56 grams) of each chocolate per person.

THE PROPER ENVIRONMENT

You can hold your chocolate tasting in an abandoned warehouse lit only by strobe lights, but the best place to taste chocolate is one that isn't filled with distractions. It is easier to focus and concentrate without, for example, bossa nova blaring in the background, regardless of how much (and how loud) you like bossa nova.

You also want to make sure that the environment and the chocolate are at the proper temperature, ideally 66 to 74°F (19 to 23°C). Temperatures much outside this range can negatively affect the perception of both the texture and the taste of the chocolate. Leaving the chocolate out in the room where it will be eaten for an hour, making sure to keep it away from heat, humidity, and direct sunlight, will bring the chocolate to room temperature.

While I can't think of a *bad* time to eat chocolate, if you want to truly taste it you should indulge when your palate is rested and at its peak. For many people this is late morning, several hours after breakfast and before lunch, or in the late afternoon, several hours after lunch and before dinner.

This is the schedule that works best for me on days when I know I will be reviewing and rating chocolate. At least two hours before I start tasting, I make sure to brush and floss my teeth extra thoroughly (and rinse extremely well) to remove any food particles that might change the chemistry of my mouth.

Most situations don't lend themselves to either the schedule or the discipline that a professional taster might require. Choose a time that works best for you and a setting that's relaxing but allows you to concentrate. I hold the majority of my tasting classes after dinner, so my students could have ingested anything from a Big Mac to a cocktail or three before they show up and I would never know. I do suggest that you refrain from drinking too much alcohol before a chocolate tasting, informal or otherwise, and if you do drink try to stay away from spirits, which will seriously dull the taste buds. You should also try to make sure that you allow at least some time after a meal to rest the palate and that you cleanse your palate thoroughly before that first bite of chocolate.

WHAT TO USE TO CLEAR YOUR PALATE WHEN TASTING

It's no less important in chocolate tasting than it is in wine tasting to start with a clean slate and to return to a clean slate between tastes. In wine tasting, the palate cleanser of choice is usually plain old water, sometimes white bread: the idea is to simply rinse out or absorb the previous wine before tasting the next one. The purpose of cleansing the palate during a chocolate tasting, on the other hand, is to remove as much of the previous chocolate's fat and fat-soluble compounds from your mouth as possible,

Chocolate for Breakfast Anyone?

Chloé Doutre-Roussel, the author of *The Chocolate Connoisseur*, likes to start tasting very early in the morning just after she wakes up and before she has anything to eat or drink. While I certainly would never discourage anyone over the age of ten from eating chocolate before breakfast, it's not exactly a practical time for most people—and definitely not convenient for group tastings or social gatherings. Choose whatever time and location will be most enjoyable for you and your friends, but before you hold your tasting see my tips below on cleansing your palate.

as they will have an impact on what is being tasted next. Fats are a little trickier to rid your mouth of than wine.

So how do you cleanse your chocolate-tasting palate? The answer to this question is the subject of a lot of controversy, with many different beverages and foods being offered up as the best.

Beverage options. I usually recommend using beverages to cleanse the palate when tasting chocolate, simply because they require less advance preparation than foods. Following are some of the ones I have found to be most effective.

1. Cool (not cold) plain water with lemon or lime slices;
2. Cool (not cold) carbonated mineral water or seltzer (with or without lemon or lime slices); and
3. Warm (not hot) Japanese green matcha tea.

Add a few lemon or lime slices to a pitcher of water (without ice, because cold water will deaden the taste buds); the acidity and some of the pectin from the fruit infuses the water, improving its effectiveness as a palate cleanser without flavoring it too much.

With carbonated water, it is the mechanical action of the bubbles that helps cleanse the mouth; adding slices of citrus enhances the cleansing. Avoid mineral waters with lots of dissolved salts, because those have strong flavors that can interfere with the taste of the chocolate. Club soda should also be avoided, because it has salt. You don't need to use expensive imported carbonated mineral waters; plain old supermarket seltzer is fine. (Spend your money on the chocolate!) If you want to make a presentation, get a home soda siphon and make the seltzer yourself.

Of all of the beverage options, my favorite is warm green matcha tea, which is fairly bitter and astringent. The bitterness counteracts the sweetness of the chocolate, and the compounds that make it astringent (drying) do a great job of cleaning the mouth. Only small sips are needed, as the tea clears out the mouth very quickly. Good matcha can be very expensive; check your local gourmet food store, Asian grocer, or online. However, there are relatively inexpensive instant green tea powders available that do almost as good a job at palate cleansing. If the cost of good matcha is prohibitive, you might also try genmaicha, which is a green tea made with toasted rice.

Food options. Following are some foods I have found to be effective palate cleansers. If you are scandalized to see Wonder Bread on the list, remember that these are not *snacks*; you are using them to cleanse your palate for the main event, which is the chocolate.

1. Unsalted blue corn tortilla chips (which are usually coarser than yellow or white corn chips and therefore do a better job of mechanically clearing the mouth);
2. Unsalted saltine crackers;
3. Plain white bread (for example, Wonder Bread) with the crusts removed; and
4. Very thin slices of tart apple (for example, Granny Smith).

If you want to truly taste chocolate, you should indulge when your palate is rested and at its peak. For many people, this is either late morning or late afternoon.

With food, the principal mechanism for clearing the mouth is mechanical: fiber in the food scours the mouth, and any fats left in the mouth stick to the fibers. Of all the food options, the last one, a thin slice of Granny Smith (or similar) apple, is my favorite. Apple slices have fiber and pectin and acidity, which, when combined, do a very effective job of cleansing the palate, and can be cut in very small slices so they won't contribute as much to a feeling of fullness. Their texture and taste add variety to the tasting process and freshen up the palate.

Offer a pitcher of cool still or sparkling water for sipping after eating the apple slice (or whatever food you choose) to complete the cleansing process.

KEEPING A TASTING JOURNAL: "MY FAVORITE CHOCOLATE IS . . . "

I suggest you keep a journal of your tasting experiences to help you remember what you've tasted. It's also useful if and when you decide to retaste a chocolate you've tasted in the past. After retasting, you can review what you thought of the chocolate the first time you tasted it. It's interesting to see how your perceptions change as you taste more and more fine chocolates.

I use a form like the one on the facing page to record my impressions of the chocolates I taste. It includes a space for you to rate your chocolates; see Rating Your Chocolate: From Ordinary to Extraordinary, page 44. You might want to make a couple dozen copies of this form and put them in a binder, or just use it as a general guide when jotting your notes in a blank book. If you're having friends over for a tasting, have some extra copies of this form or a few small notebooks on hand so that they can start their own chocolate tasting journals.

CHOCOPHILE CHECKLIST

DESCRIPTION (manufacturer/name/type/percentage):

NOTES (where purchased, cost, other chocolates tasted in this session, etc.):

INITIAL IMPRESSIONS (aroma, appearance, snap):

TASTE IMPRESSIONS (initial, middle, short, long):

TEXTURE IMPRESSIONS:

OVERALL IMPRESSIONS:

RATING:

Great chocolates balance
all of the sense elements
in a harmonious whole.

TASTING A BAR OF CHOCOLATE WITH ALL YOUR SENSES

✴

You've invited some chocolate-loving friends over. You've set out the Granny Smiths and cool lemon water or brewed a pot of matcha tea. And you've artfully displayed your latest chocolate haul on the table, all of it still untouched—what self-control you've shown!—beautiful embossed, gilded wrappers intact. Now that the stage has been set, it's time to learn how to taste chocolate using every sensual tool at your disposal.

The best chocolates engage all of our senses. Sight, touch, smell, taste, and even (to a lesser extent) hearing all have roles to play in our enjoyment of chocolate. Great chocolates balance all of the sense elements in a harmonious whole that is greater than the sum of the individual parts.

STEP 1: SMELL THE CHOCOLATE

Immediately upon opening the wrapper or the package, smell the chocolate. Bring the chocolate close to your nose and breathe in deeply several times.

What you are smelling for is:

1. The intensity of the chocolate smell (Is it subtle, or strong and clear?);
2. The clarity of the chocolate smell (Do you smell any scents other than chocolate, especially vanilla?); and
3. The sweetness of the chocolate smell (Does the impression of sweetness overwhelm the intensity and clarity of the other smells?).

In addition to chocolate, several other scents are common when you first smell a bar or box of chocolate. Depending on where the beans came from, the type of chocolate, and how the chocolate was made, you might detect scents that remind you of:

CHOCOPHILE FACT
The only way to become an accomplished chocolate taster is to taste a lot of chocolate.

✴

Vanilla

*

Fruit

*

Toast

*

Smoke

*

Bitterness

*

Spice

*

Milk

*

Earth

- Vanilla
- Fruit (red, citrus, tropical)
- Toast (toasted bread, roasted nuts)
- Smoke (smoked over a fire)
- Bitterness (burnt)
- Spice (cinnamon)
- Milk (cooked sugar, caramel) and/or
- Earth (wood, fungi) smells

If the smell of vanilla is very strong, it may mean that artificial vanilla (ethyl vanillin) has been used to cover up an undesirable aspect of the chocolate. When it is used in high proportions, ethyl vanillin can also have an artificial, slightly acrid chemical odor, which is definitely not desirable.

Sometimes a chocolate can smell overly sweet. This is also not generally desirable unless you happen to like very sweet chocolate. Chocolate can also smell "light" (the aromas are high up in the nose) or heavy (the aromas are low in the nose).

While smelling the chocolate, especially when you're new to the tasting process, it's not important to be able to precisely identify and catalog all of the different scents you encounter. What is most important is to characterize a general impression based on the broad scent categories listed above. It's okay to identify the smell of the chocolate as earthy and smoky; you don't have to stretch to identify the earthy smell as "peaty" or the type of wood smoke as "mesquite."

If you are having trouble identifying any scents, lightly rub your thumb against the chocolate to warm it up—a trick that chocolate professionals use. As the chocolate warms up, the cocoa butter melts slightly, releasing more aromatic components and making it easier to smell faint scents. Once the chocolate has been warmed up, bring it (not your thumb) close to your nose and breathe in deeply—it should be easier to get a strong smell impression this way.

When tasting wine, one of the first things you might do is raise your glass and note the color and consistency of the liquid in it. It's not that different with chocolate, though of course you're looking for other attributes. The more beautiful the piece of chocolate is, the more pleasure you will probably derive from eating it, but visual appearance can also tell you a lot about the quality of the chocolate and what to expect when you reach step 4 and finally get to taste it.

The Color of Chocolate

If you take a close look at two different bars of chocolate, chances are you will be able to discern slight differences in their colors. Some chocolates are warmer (red-brown) and some chocolates are cooler (purple-brown), and there are also differences in value (lightness or darkness). With very few exceptions, however, there are too many variables associated with chocolate manufacturing to infer much of anything about the taste or quality of a chocolate from its color. One of those exceptions is chocolate that is purported to be made from pure Porcelana Criollo beans. The name *Porcelana* is derived from the Spanish word for porcelain and refers to the fresh beans' pale interior, which is almost white.

Among the rarest beans in the world, the Porcelana bean requires delicate handling, especially when it comes to roasting, as it is very easy to over-roast and burn these beans, masking their delicate flavors. If you are eating a bar made of pure Porcelana cacao, the bar should be red-brown and fairly light. If the Porcelana bar you're eating does not match this description it's because it's not made with pure Porcelana, and/or the beans have not been processed properly after harvesting, and/or the beans have been over-roasted. Whatever the reason, this means that you will not be enjoying the true taste of the Porcelana beans—and you really should taste them sometime.

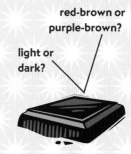

red-brown or purple-brown?

light or dark?

Cocoa butter bloom

Sugar bloom

Pinholes

When you look at a piece (that is, a bar) of dark chocolate, you are looking for a surface appearance that ranges from a matte sheen to glossy depending on the type of chocolate and the techniques used. The surface appearance provides indicators of good technique in tempering and proper storage and handling. If the surface has a flat appearance it may indicate lower-quality processing, though milk chocolates, in general, are not as shiny as dark chocolates.

A white, powdery-looking coating on chocolate is an indication of cocoa butter bloom, which means that the chocolate has been improperly stored. Depending on how bad the bloom is, and how long the bloom has been on the chocolate, taste and texture can both be affected and the chocolate is not at its best.

An irregular white coating with what looks like the remnants of sugar crystals is an indication of sugar bloom, which means that moisture condensed on the chocolate, drawing some of the sugar to the surface. The texture of the chocolate is ruined, and you should have no expectations of a quality experience should you decide to eat it anyway.

Look for pinholes in the surface. When chocolate is poured into a mold, air bubbles sometimes form. The molds are shaken or put onto a vibration table to force the air bubbles out of the chocolate. If the mold is not shaken properly these air bubbles can remain resulting in pinholes on the surface of the chocolate. Usually they are just unsightly and don't affect the taste or texture of the chocolate, but they do indicate that the molding process was rushed—something you wouldn't expect of a top-level chocolate maker.

STEP 3: TOUCH THE CHOCOLATE AND LISTEN TO ITS "SNAP"

The next step is to break the chocolate into two pieces by snapping it. (This step does not really apply to confections; don't break a truffle with a liquid caramel center unless you really want to make a mess.)

With dark chocolate, the "snap" (as it is called) should both feel and sound crisp but not brittle. If the snap is brittle it's usually a sign that the chocolate might be very old or that it has been stored improperly. Brittle chocolate won't be pleasant to eat (the texture in the mouth will be dry and sandy, not smooth and creamy), but it's probably possible to rehabilitate the chocolate for cooking and baking by melting and tempering it again.

If the snap is not crisp, it's probably a sign that you're eating dark chocolate with fats other than cocoa butter in it, milk chocolate, or chocolate that is too warm and has become soft. If the environment is not too warm—that is, it's less than 78°F (26°C)—and you're eating dark chocolate, you may want to look closely at the label to see if there are any non–cocoa butter fats in the chocolate. If there are (butter oil is a common example of an ingredient that might appear on the label), it will have a negative effect on other sensory aspects of the chocolate, especially the texture of the chocolate in your mouth as it melts.

Some Cocoa Butters Are Harder than Others

All fats are mixtures of triglycerides, which are chemicals composed of three fatty acids. In cocoa butter, triglycerides containing the fatty acids oleic acid, stearic acid, and palmitic acid comprise over 95 percent of the total fatty acid content. Because cocoa butters made from beans from different growing regions may contain triglycerides with different fatty acid ratios, and because cocoa butters melt and solidify at different rates depending on their exact chemical makeup, some cocoa butters are "harder" than others—they feel crisper, perhaps chewier, and aren't perceived as melting as smoothly as cocoa butters that are "softer." Most chocolate is made from blends of beans from different parts of the world plus additional cocoa butter (and, often, non–cocoa butter fats), so the chemical composition of the resultant mix of fats is very complex. Some combinations melt easily and are perceived as smooth and creamy. Other combinations are hard and chewy, don't melt as easily, and can be perceived as being "waxy."

Costa Rica

Ghana

Sri Lanka

Congratulations on getting this far without giving in to the almost primal urge to stuff all of the chocolate in your mouth immediately after opening the wrapper or box. Okay, it's probably only been less than a minute, but it really does *seem* like a long time. Now it's time to taste.

Almost time to taste, that is. There is actually a great deal of controversy about how to eat chocolate and how much to eat.

How you eat the chocolate primarily has an effect on texture: chewing it delivers a different texture than letting it melt on your tongue (believe it or not, scientists have studied the physics of this phenomenon).

So. Should you chew it or let it melt? The answer is simple: both. As you place a piece of chocolate in your mouth, breathe in to get the aroma of the chocolate working in your nose as it starts to melt in your mouth.

How Much Chocolate Is the Right Amount to Taste?

No, this isn't a trick question, and the answer isn't "As much as you can fit in your mouth." There are some people who claim that it is impossible to get a true sense of the flavor and texture of a piece of chocolate unless the portion is at least one ounce (28 grams). (For comparison's sake, that's the size of a square of supermarket baking chocolate. Most tasting squares are $^1/_5$ to $^1/_4$ ounce [5 to 7 grams], so these tasters are eating four or five tasting squares of each chocolate.)

When I'm evaluating several chocolates in a sitting, I tend to like to taste smaller portions more in line with the size of a standard tasting square, about $^1/_4$ ounce (7 grams), in two separate tastes, for a total of about $^1/_2$ ounce (14 grams) per chocolate. These smaller portion sizes can affect the perception of texture when you're chewing, but I often find it hard to tell if the differences I'm sensing are due to the thickness of the bar or the actual texture of the chocolate.

Smell is an important part of taste, after all. When the chocolate is in your mouth, chew it three to five times. As you are chewing, pay attention to the textural sensations and try to characterize them. Is the chocolate sandy or dry? Chewy without being waxy? Chewy and waxy? Smooth? Are there any other textures such as sugar crystals or large particles of cocoa solids? Do you like or dislike these textures?

After you've chewed the chocolate, gather the mass against the roof of your mouth and let it melt. As it melts there are a few things you should do:

- "Cluck" (sometimes called "guppying") by pursing your lips and drawing air into your mouth and over the chocolate on your tongue. The increase in airflow warms and oxygenates the chocolate and enhances your ability to discern faint smells. (This technique is not as off the wall as it sounds: many wine tasters will suck a bit of the wine through their front teeth to oxygenate it.)
- With your mouth and eyes closed, slowly and deliberately breathe in deeply through your nose, concentrating on what you smell. Do this several times—as often as you like, in fact—until you are satisfied that you can recognize all the different scents in the chocolate.
- Take a little bit of the melted chocolate and "worry" it between the tip of your tongue and the base of your upper teeth in order to discern if there is any grittiness at all in the chocolate.

As with the earlier smelling step, it's not all that important that you be able to precisely identify your impressions of the flavor. Generalizations (smoky, earthy, sweet) are okay, though if you can be more precise that's good. It's just as important to be able to say which sense impressions you *like* and which you *don't* like.

Cluck

＊

Breathe

＊

"Worry"

IDENTIFYING YOUR TASTING ZONES

✳

CHOCOPHILE FACT

"Better" choco-
late doesn't
necessarily
mean more
robust flavor.
The most prized
cocoa beans
make chocolate
with the most
subtle, nuanced
flavors.

✳

There are four separate tasting "zones" to pay attention to. These are not based on areas of your mouth or tongue; they are temporal, or based on time.

INITIAL TASTE

The initial taste is the one you get as soon as you put the chocolate in your mouth. The primary taste sensations during this taste zone will be fruitiness, bitterness, intensity of chocolate flavor, and sweetness.

MIDDLE TASTE

As you are chewing the chocolate and letting it melt on your tongue, you will be able to detect many flavor nuances, such as woody, earthy, tobacco, olives, fruits, herbal, floral, and so on. If there is any astringent effect from the chocolate (from tannins, which cause a dry sensation in the mouth) you will begin to feel it now, often under the sides of the tongue or at the back of the mouth. The most expensive chocolates are going to be the most subtle—that is, those made from Criollo beans, and especially Porcelana, which will never have a robust bitter chocolate taste.

SHORT AFTERTASTE

The short aftertaste is where any additional astringency will show up and you will be able to start to feel on your tongue if there are any fats in the chocolate that should not be there. For example, butter oil will often leave a pasty feeling on the tongue. A good chocolate will have a "clean and clear" aftertaste and texture, which means that the chocolate and its fats clear the mouth quickly. The strength of the flavor that is left, and how long it remains in the mouth, is a good indicator of the quality of the beans and the skill of the chocolate maker. It is usually in the short aftertaste that the chemical taste of artificial vanilla really starts to become apparent, as do any chemical overtones from sugar substitutes.

The long aftertaste (more than thirty seconds after all traces of the chocolate have left your mouth) is really the indicator of quality chocolate. There should be no off tastes in your mouth at all. Sometimes, an acrid chemical taste reveals itself that is not at all apparent in the first three phases of tasting. Most people don't eat chocolate this slowly, and drinking or eating something (such as more chocolate) before the long aftertaste has a chance to show up will disguise these off tastes completely.

FLAVORS COMMONLY FOUND IN CHOCOLATE

❋

The following flavor descriptors are part of the language of chocolate. Depending on your own ability to taste, at first you might (for example) get just a spicy impression, or you might be able to identify a particular spice.

- *Spicy*
  Vanilla, Asian spices, cinnamon, cloves, licorice
- *Nutty*
  Macadamia nuts, hazelnuts, almonds, cashews, Brazil nuts
- *Roasted*
  Black tea, coffee/espresso, marzipan, caramel, caramelized sugar, roasted almond
- *Dairy*
  Butter, cream, milk, cheese

- *Fruity*
  Apricot, red berries (raspberries, currants), plums, cherries, citrus, dried fruits, fig, tropical/exotic fruits
- *Flowery*
  Jasmine, orange blossom, rose
- *Earthy*
  Mushrooms, green tomato, truffles, wood
- *Other*
  Sour, tobacco, bread, honey, beeswax, smoke, no. 2 pencil

CHOCOLATE FLAVOR PROFILE COMPONENTS

The flavor components of a chocolate can be expressed on a scale of 0 (weak) to 10 (strong) and then charted on a "spider graph," a visual representation of the flavor profile of a chocolate.

These graphs are becoming increasingly popular with chocolate manufacturers and, as you expand your chocolate horizons, it is likely that you will run across a graph similar to the examples below.

When looking at these graphs it is important to pay attention to whether or not milk or dark chocolate is being profiled, as the component axes are not the same. Also, chocolate manufacturers each tend to have their own versions of these graphs that either use different axes or place the axes in a different order.

With practice a careful examination of a spider graph will give you a general impression of the overall flavor characteristics of a particular chocolate. However, you can't rely on a spider graph for a thorough description of the flavor of a chocolate, as the following examples demonstrate.

The flavor profile of the dark chocolate plotted in the left-hand graph can be summarized as follows: "well-balanced combination of coffee and plum; distinct cocoa aromas; aromas of orange blossom and cinnamon; light sweet raisin bouquet; long final sensation." The flavor profile of the milk chocolate plotted in the right-hand graph includes "full-bodied milk/cream taste; subtle notes of honey and caramel; delicate roasting; vanilla taste."

DARK CHOCOLATE TASTE PROFILE

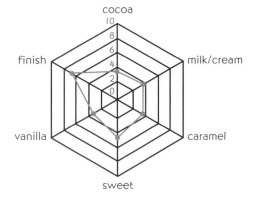

MILK CHOCOLATE TASTE PROFILE

TASTING TRUFFLES WITH ALL YOUR SENSES

✳

The procedure for tasting truffles is a little different from the one used for tasting bars of straight chocolate, and there are slight variations for the different types of truffles: hand rolled, enrobed, and shell molded.

SIGHT

At first you might be attracted by the sheen of a luxurious ballotin box, by the artistry of a brightly colored transfer (made using colored cocoa butter designs printed on acetate), or by the intricacy of a delicate mold. But it is important to look past the outer trappings of packaging and decoration because that can tell you a lot about the chocolate you are about to eat.

Look for pinholes in the surface of a shell-molded truffle or cracks in the surface of enrobed or hand-rolled truffles. Pinholes are an indication that the molding process was rushed. Cracks are either an indication of improper technique (for example, if the center of a truffle is too cold when it is enrobed, it cracks when it warms up) or rough handling (the box may have been dropped during shipment). Tiny pinholes are just unsightly, but if a pinhole or crack is big or deep enough it can weaken the shell and cause the truffle either to leak or to allow air and bacteria to get into the center, spoiling it prematurely.

If you are eating a shell-molded or enrobed confection, take a look at the bottom of the piece because it can tell you a lot about the chocolatier's attention to detail. Are the bottoms smooth and glossy? Do the pieces look like they were created by a skilled craftsperson who takes pride in each and every chocolate, or are there obvious visible imperfections? (That fellow over in the corner of the chocolate shop methodically turning over each truffle and examining the bottom? Chocolate professional.)

SMELL

When you stick your nose into a box of great chocolate, all you should be able to smell is chocolate: rich, robust, intense, heady. Especially if the box is all pieces coated in dark chocolate, sweetness should not be the predominant smell. If you can smell the centers, the chocolatier has used too much flavoring, probably essential oils or artificial flavorings.

TASTE AND TEXTURE

The *truffe nature*, a simple hand-rolled ball of dark ganache dusted with cocoa powder, may be the purest expression of truffle making. Its simplicity is deceptive, though, as a delicate hand is required to balance the elegant taste and ethereal texture of the ganache with the dusky intensity of the cocoa powder. However, when tasting a chocolate truffle of any style, chocolate should be the first flavor and last flavor you taste. Any other flavoring that has been added to the chocolate—mint, raspberry, or what have you—should be front and center only during the middle taste and short aftertaste.

One of the primary characteristics that distinguishes various styles of chocolate confectionery is how the flavors added to the chocolate are expressed. In what I think of as the "French style," the flavors tend to be subtle, elusive, and hard to identify. In "Belgian-style" chocolates, the flavors are easier to identify but the overall flavor profile tends to be sweeter, even in dark pieces. In "American-style" chocolates, the flavors are very easy to identify and often overpower the chocolate. Sometime in 2003, a "nouvelle American style" appeared, in which the taste of the chocolate is of primary importance, but the added flavors are more "forward" and more easily identifiable than is typically the case in French-style chocolates.

"Ganache is not only chocolate and cream, it is what you do with those two ingredients after careful study and mastery."

—Robert Linxe, from *La Maison du Chocolat: Transcendent Desserts by the Legendary Chocolatier*

A FIELD GUIDE TO TRUFFLES

**Truffles are made using one of three methods.
(Terms in bold are defined in the Glossary, page 145).**

HAND-ROLLED TRUFFLE: The center filling, typically **ganache**, is shaped by hand: the ganache is formed into portions, with a spoon, scoop, or piping bag, which are quickly rolled between the palms of the hands to give them their final (usually spherical) shape. These ganache balls can then be dipped in chocolate (enrobing them), or they can be rolled in cocoa powder (the classic *truffe nature*) or other coatings such as crushed nuts.

ENROBED TRUFFLE: The center filling, often a **ganache**, **caramel**, or **praliné**, supports a thin chocolate coating. Enrobed truffles are made by spreading the filling into a sheet of even thickness and allowing it to cool. The filling is cut into equal-sized pieces using a device called a **guitar**. The pieces are then ready to be covered with chocolate, a process called enrobing. This can be done manually by dipping the pieces one at a time into tempered chocolate, or with the aid of an enrobing machine.

SHELL-MOLDED TRUFFLE: A thin outer shell of chocolate supports the filling, often a **ganache**, **caramel**, or **praliné**. The shell is made by pouring **tempered** chocolate into cavities (shaped depressions) in a mold and then allowing the chocolate to set for a short period of time, forming a solid coating on the inside of the mold. When the shell is set, the filling is poured or piped into the hollow center of the mold. After it sets, tempered chocolate is poured over the top to seal the truffle and form a flat bottom when the truffles are turned out of the mold.

What's Your Pleasure: Belgian or Nouvelle American?

Here are four major styles of chocolate making, each with its own distinctive characteristics.

Belgian style: Chocolate in the Belgian style (and this includes many Swiss chocolates) is lighter and sweeter than chocolate made in the French style. In confections, the centers are often quite sweet, with pronounced flavors that are equally as important as the chocolate, and there is an emphasis on intricate shell-molding techniques.

French style: Chocolate in the French style (and this includes most Spanish and Italian chocolates) is darker, less sweet, and more bitter than chocolate made in the Belgian style. With confections, the centers tend to be less sweet, and the added flavors are often subtle to the point of being hard to distinguish: the taste of the chocolate tends to be more important. There is an emphasis on enrobed techniques.

American style: There is nothing subtle about American-style chocolates. Centers tend to be very sweet, and the added flavors often overpower the flavor of the chocolate itself.

Nouvelle American style: Created by European chocolatiers working in America, the nouvelle American style of chocolate merges the best of the French and Belgian styles of chocolate making. Added flavors tend to be clear and distinct, further forward than in the French style but not as dominant as in the Belgian style. Centers tend to be less sweet, and there is no particular emphasis on either shell molding or enrobing techniques.

The thickness of a truffle's outer shell has an enormous impact on your perception of its taste and texture. There's something irresistible about the way a very thin shell cracks as you bite into it, giving access to the fine ganache center. Thick shells are much easier to produce consistently than very thin ones are, and they serve to slow the penetration of oxygen into the center, increasing the truffle's shelf life. Thin shells are a sign of the chocolatier's mastery of technique, but they also mean that the truffle must be eaten soon after manufacture. In general, the more you pay for a chocolate, the more entitled you are to expect a thinner shell, a more consistent thickness of shell, fewer visible defects, and a better balance among its flavors and textures.

RATING YOUR CHOCOLATE:
FROM ORDINARY TO EXTRAORDINARY

✳

Now that you know how to taste chocolate and record your impressions of it, the next step is rating it. Refer back to the rating form, page 27.

I recommend using a rating system that focuses on whether or not you would buy or eat the chocolate again. When tasting chocolates with a group of people, using the following four ratings can be a lot of fun: the ratings make the experience personal and invite comparisons among different chocolates.

↑

Great

✳

Good

✳

Ordinary

✳

Bad

↓

- *Great chocolate.* If I could arrange it, this is one of the only chocolates I would eat. When someone gives me chocolate as a gift, this is one of the ones I want. If I really wanted to impress someone, I would buy this to give to him or her. I would share this chocolate only with someone who was really, really, *really* nice to me.

- *Good chocolate.* There's a lot I like about this chocolate, and I would spend my own money on it. If someone gave it to me as a gift I would definitely eat it and I might even share it with my significant other/best friend/relative/boss—if he or she was nice to me.

- *Ordinary chocolate.* There are some things about this chocolate I like, but I wouldn't spend my own money on it. I might eat it if someone gave it to me as a gift, or I might regift it (and I wouldn't feel *too* bad about giving it away).

- *Bad chocolate.* I do not like this chocolate at all and I would not eat it even if it were given to me as a gift. It's so bad, in fact, that I would only regift it to someone I really, really didn't like.

This is not the FDA's food pyramid. It's actually a way to very quickly and easily figure out what you do and don't like about chocolate, in order to develop your palate and to understand and communicate what you are tasting.

It is very difficult for most people to taste a piece of chocolate and express exactly what they are tasting. It's far easier to compare two chocolates:

- This one is sweeter than that one. I like chocolate that is less sweet.
- The milk in this one has a caramel taste, and that one doesn't. I like the caramel taste.
- This one has a lot of fruitiness in it—red fruit, I think, but I can't tell which one. That one has a rich, earthy taste. I prefer the earthy taste to the fruity taste.
- This one is 85 percent cocoa and that one is 70 percent cocoa. I don't really like the 85 percent—it's too intense for me.

To develop your own tasting pyramid, start with either four, eight, or sixteen chocolates with similar characteristics. You should create separate pyramids for dark chocolate, milk chocolate, and specialty chocolate (chocolate with other ingredients in it, flavored chocolate, truffles, and so on).

Arrange the chocolates in pairs for the base of your pyramid; you can be as arbitrary or deliberate as you like. Tasting the chocolates in pairs, describe the chocolates in relationship to each other, using phrases like the bulleted ones above. Try to come up with at least three comparisons for each pair of chocolates, and write down your impressions of which chocolate in each pair tastes better to you and why (you can fill out a form like the one on page 27 to keep track of your notes).

Do this for all the pairs of chocolate in the base of your pyramid. As you choose your favorite from each pair, move it to the next level of the pyramid. Put the ones you didn't like as much into a separate pile off to the side.

Repeat for the next row in your chocolate pyramid, comparing the chocolates in pairs, recording your impressions, then selecting your favorite from each pair. Repeat the process until you reach an overall favorite for that pyramid.

Pair 1   Pair 2

Favorite

Now look at your tasting notes for all of your favorites. Chances are good that you'll see a recognizable pattern in your choices, the pattern that describes your personal chocolate preferences. If you don't see a pattern (and you might not see one right away if you started with only four or eight chocolates), just repeat the pyramid tasting starting with different pairings. Quite quickly it will become very clear to you what characteristics you respond positively to, what you are neutral about, and what you really don't care for.

Even if you do see a pattern after running through the pyramid only once, go ahead and rearrange the pairings at the base of the pyramid and taste them all again. Besides the fact that you get to keep eating chocolate until it's all gone, a second (or third) run-through really is instructive. The choice of pairings can completely change your impressions of a particular chocolate.

After you've run through a couple of different pyramids for milk and dark chocolate, you will have a very strong idea of what you like and what you don't like about each type. Armed with that knowledge, you can face any new tasting situation with aplomb. •

2.

How Cacao Becomes Chocolate

THE MAGICAL TRANSFORMATION, STEP-BY-STEP

SURE. ✳ It's less sexy than sampling a square of 85 percent from an up-and-coming chocolate maker or organizing a truffle tasting, but an appreciation of the chocolate-making process is as invaluable to a chocolate lover's enjoyment as an understanding of the winemaking process is to a wine connoisseur. A wine lover can certainly drink a lot of excellent wine—and enjoy it immensely—without knowing that Burgundy reds are made from Pinot Noir grapes or that budget Chardonnays are aged not in oak barrels but in steel barrels to which wood chips have been added, but he's probably paying more for his wine, drinking a lot of poor wine, and in all likelihood not enjoying the good wines nearly as much as he might. The same is true for chocolate lovers: knowing where the stuff comes from and how it's made will help you choose the best of it at the best prices, and will enhance your enjoyment of the fine chocolates you come across wherever you travel.

Chocolate as we know it today is one of the glorious achievements of the Industrial Revolution. Until the widespread availability of machinery that could refine cocoa and sugar particles until they were extremely fine, most chocolate was consumed in beverage form. Cookbooks from the Colonial American era and earlier include recipes for chocolate ices, ice creams, baked puddings, and cakes. Prior to the mid-1800s, any "eating" chocolate, which would have been molded into small bars or other shapes, would have been very gritty and dry, tasting nothing like the luxuriously unctuous treats we take for granted today. (If you're curious about how these early chocolates tasted, there are companies that specialize in making chocolate using antique recipes and techniques.)

Other books do an excellent job of recounting the history of chocolate (see Resources, page 154), so I won't attempt to tell the entire story here. I'll only say that many inventions and innovations over the course of nearly a century led to the widespread availability of inexpensive, smooth, and creamy chocolate bars.

One hallmark of industrial—as opposed to artisanal—products is standardization. Wine comes from an artisan tradition, and the most valued and respected wines remain true to those practices, including an emphasis on handcrafting from start to finish using local ingredients. The same is true for fine cheeses, olive oils, and many other gourmet foods. Chocolate came from an artisan tradition but lost contact with much of its heritage when it became an industrial food product. One curious result of this evolution is that, even with artisanal chocolates, the primary ingredient (cocoa) is grown somewhere other than where the chocolate is made.

Following is an outline of all the steps in the chocolate-making process, starting with the cultivation of cacao trees and ending with the molding of chocolate into bars or bon bons for you to eat. At first glance, you may think this flow chart is a bit of a yawn and wonder how the information contained in it is relevant to your enjoyment of chocolate. I'll admit that flow charts aren't as appealing as, say, a molten chocolate cake, but read on and you'll learn the significance of each of these steps to chocolate lovers.

How Chocolate Became Delectable: A Timeline of Key Inventions

1828: The cocoa butter press is patented by Coenraad van Houten in Holland.

1879: A practical way to make milk chocolate is developed by Henri Nestlé and Daniel Peter in Switzerland.

1847: Extra cocoa butter is added to refined chocolate liquor to improve viscosity (making chocolate easier to pour and mold) by the Fry family in England.

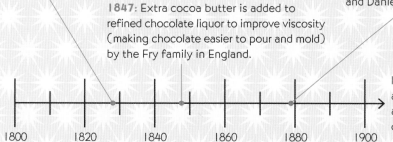

Early twentieth century: Practical and affordable refrigeration and air-conditioning systems are developed for commercial use.

Mid- to late nineteenth century: A wide range of specialized chocolate manufacturing machinery is developed and made widely available. This includes the conche, a machine invented by Swiss chocolatier Rudolphe Lindt in the late 1870s to help make the texture of chocolate smoother and the taste less acidic.

How Cacao Becomes Chocolate

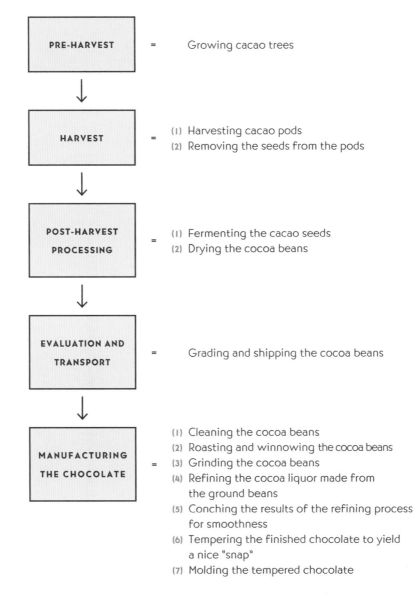

PRE-HARVEST = Growing cacao trees

HARVEST =
(1) Harvesting cacao pods
(2) Removing the seeds from the pods

POST-HARVEST PROCESSING =
(1) Fermenting the cacao seeds
(2) Drying the cocoa beans

EVALUATION AND TRANSPORT = Grading and shipping the cocoa beans

MANUFACTURING THE CHOCOLATE =
(1) Cleaning the cocoa beans
(2) Roasting and winnowing the cocoa beans
(3) Grinding the cocoa beans
(4) Refining the cocoa liquor made from the ground beans
(5) Conching the results of the refining process for smoothness
(6) Tempering the finished chocolate to yield a nice "snap"
(7) Molding the tempered chocolate

An appreciation of the chocolate-making process is as invaluable to a chocolate lover's enjoyment as an understanding of the winemaking process is to a wine connoisseur.

BEFORE THE HARVEST:
HOW AND WHERE CACAO TREES ARE GROWN

*

To start at the very beginning, all chocolate is made from the seeds of the fruit of the cacao tree (*Theobroma cacao*, or *T. cacao*). Although the cacao tree, a tropical plant, originated in the Amazon River basin (and it is thought that the ancestors of the plant may have originated on what is now the African continent when it was a part of Gondwanaland), today cacao is grown around the world in a band that extends roughly twenty degrees north and south of the equator.

Transatlantic trade in cacao between Mexico and Spain started taking place by the mid-1500s. Not long thereafter, as European countries looked to exploit their colonial holdings around the world, cacao begun to spread from its New World home, first to southeast Asian colonies including the Philippines, Malaysia, and Indonesia. Over the next two hundred and fifty years, cacao came to be grown in Madagascar, Sri Lanka (Ceylon), India, Papua New Guinea, Fiji, and throughout the South Pacific.

Although western Africa now produces over 80 percent of the world's cacao, it is a relative newcomer; the Portuguese planted the first recorded cacao there in the early 1800s. The Ivory Coast and Ghana, who together produce about 70 percent of the world's supply of cacao (virtually all the forastero), did not begin production until the mid- to late 1800s. (For further information, see Maps of the Most Important Cocoa-Producing Countries, pages 140–144.)

The genetics of the cacao tree determine the potential for flavor of the chocolate that is made from its beans. All of the subsequent steps in harvesting, post-harvest processing, and chocolate manufacturing serve to bring out the flavor that is inherent in the genetics of the cacao. This

When Does Cacao Become Cocoa?

There is no universally accepted answer to this question. The word *cocoa* came into common use as an easy-to-pronounce alternative to *cacao* when the latter was misspelled in an early translation. I prefer to use the term cacao when referring to the tree, pods, or live seeds (up through the harvesting process) and cocoa once fermentation is complete and the seeds can no longer germinate (the start of the post-harvesting process). The ability to germinate is the technical difference between a seed and a bean, so you can say that cacao seeds become cocoa beans during fermentation. From there, the cocoa beans are dried, graded, and shipped—then it's time to make some chocolate.

cacao

cocoa

bit of information is critical to your understanding—and enhanced enjoyment—of whatever chocolate you eat. So, you'll want to start paying attention to the type and origin of the cacao used to make your chocolate. (See How to Read the Ingredients Label of a Bar of Chocolate, page 102, to learn how and where this information is indicated.)

When I first began traveling in what's known as the "Cocoa Belt," I quickly learned that the cacao tree is a unique and fascinating plant in several ways. Cacao pods grow from pollinated flowers found on cushions on the trunk and branches of the cacao tree. Cacao flowers are pollinated by midges, tiny flying insects that live in the leaf litter (dead leaves, twigs, and bark) on the ground beneath the trees. Cacao trees produce thousands of flowers each year, and pods develop from the flowers that are pollinated. Hybrids occur when the pollen from flowers on one tree is deposited in flowers on another tree.

Unlike most plants, cacao flowers can be pollinated multiple times, so it is even possible to have several hybrids in the same pod. This means that when it's time to harvest the pods and begin the process that leads to the

Cacao flowers

Chocolate Trees Don't Grow in Belgium: Cacao Cultivation in the New World

Cacao, like corn (maize), tomatoes, potatoes, chilies, vanilla, and other now-common foods, herbs, and spices, was not known to Europeans until the "discovery" of the New World in the 1500s by the Spanish. The first Europeans to see cacao beans were Christopher Columbus and his crew on August 15, 1502, near the island Guanaja off the coast of modern-day Honduras. Columbus (who never tasted chocolate) and his men had no clue that these "almonds" (as they referred to them) were the most highly prized agricultural product of the most advanced civilizations in the New World.

Europeans arriving in the Americas to exploit the natural resources found there quickly came to understand the importance and value of cacao,

however, and within fifty years or so there was a thriving trade in cocoa between the Spanish colonies of the New World and Spain. While other New World crops would be successfully transplanted to European lands and quickly become mainstays of the economies and cuisines of many European cultures, cacao proved incapable of growing outside of the tropics. To this day, except for some lonely trees in botanical gardens in New York City and London, cacao is still grown in a fairly narrow band that stretches twenty degrees north and south of the equator. Cacao is grown in developing countries where the cost of labor is low, and access to transportation and refrigeration is not taken for granted.

+ 20°

0°

- 20°

creation of chocolate, cacao beans from the same tree can actually be a mix of many cacao hybrids. To compare this with winemaking: it's as if Pinot Noir grapes could be spontaneously hybridized on the vine with Riesling varietals to yield Pinot Noir and Pinot/Riesling hybrids not only growing on the same vine but in the same bunch. That would lead to significant changes in the way wines were made and marketed as it has with chocolate.

What else makes the cacao tree special? It's the only known tree that is self-regulating, meaning that it will only bring to maturity fruit that it has the resources to grow fully. Pods that the tree can't support wither away naturally, an extremely sensible adaptation that makes me think of cacao trees as smart trees.

While there are many species of cacao, only one, *T. cacao*, can be used to make chocolate. Within the *T. cacao* genus there are two main types, or varieties, of cacao trees: Criollo and Forastero. Like *T. cacao*, which is Latin, *Criollo* and *Forastero* are names that came into use only after Europeans "discovered" cacao when the Spanish first visited the New World in the 1500s.

Of the two types, Criollo (pronounced cree-YO-yo and meaning "native") trees produce the highest-quality beans. However, Criollo is a more delicate plant than Forastero, harder to grow and more susceptible to diseases, and yields fewer pods and therefore beans per tree each harvest. Forastero (pronounced fore-uh-STARE-oh and meaning "foreign") trees produce beans that are lower quality than Criollo, but they are easier to grow, hardier, and have higher yields.

A direct comparison can be made between cocoa bean and coffee bean types. Criollo can be likened to Arabica, a type of coffee plant that produces higher-quality beans and is lower yielding. In the cocoa industry, Criollo beans are considered to be "flavor" beans. Forastero can be likened to Robusta, a type of coffee plant that produces lower-quality beans but forms the majority of the crop. In the cocoa industry, Forastero beans are considered to be "bulk" beans. Forastero beans constitute the largest part of the harvest each year by far, accounting for more than 95 percent of all the cocoa beans harvested in 2004.

Another common type of cacao is a hybrid of Criollo and Forastero called Trinitario, because it was bred on the island of Trinidad. Because of their Criollo genetic heritage, Trinitarios are considered to be flavor beans,

Criollo

High

Quality

Low

Yield

*

Forastero

Low

Quality

High

Yield

more desirable for chocolate manufacturing than their bulk-bean brothers, forastero. Today, the vast majority of flavor cacao grown are Trinitario varieties. Only a very small amount of true Criollo is harvested each year.

A fourth common type of cacao, called Nacional, is native to Ecuador. The Nacional is a Forastero cacao that has many Criollo characteristics. Despite the fact that it's technically a Forastero, or bulk bean, the Nacional is considered a flavor bean. That's because it is the only cacao bean that has a name for its unique flavor, arriba, which is redolent of jasmine and orange blossom.

In addition to these four main types of beans, an uncountable number of spontaneously occurring and man-made hybrid cacao varieties exist. In general, the commercially important, spontaneously occurring hybrids that you'll want to know about are named according to the place where they grow: Ocumare (Venezuela), Esmeralda (Ecuador), Carenero (Venezuela). Man-made hybrids often have technical names like CCN-51.

Identifying cacao varieties by their external characteristics (called pheno-typing) is an art, and like most artistic endeavors it is not 100 percent accurate. As can be seen in the photograph below, pods harvested within the same small plot (in this case a backyard plot of less than half a hectare—about one and a quarter acres—in Venezuela) can display a wide variety of sizes, colors, and shapes. Maricel Presilla's book *The New Taste of Chocolate* includes a very good guide to pod identification.

To Blend or Not to Blend?

The vast majority of chocolate is blended from beans grown in different regions. Blending is usually done for one or more of the following reasons:

- **Blending is done to control cost.** In this case, the majority of the chocolate is made from bulk, or non-flavor-grade, beans. Small amounts of flavor-grade beans are added to create a specific flavor profile.
- **Blending is done to maintain consistent taste.** When this is the case, there is a target flavor profile that must be reached and beans from different regions and at different roasts are blended together in different percentages to reach the desired flavor. This is where the true art of chocolate making comes to

the fore: the chocolate maker must understand how roast affects flavor and how to use roast and bean ratios to achieve the desired result.

- **Blending is done to create favors that don't occur naturally.** Sometimes the flavor that a chocolate manufacturer seeks doesn't exist in a single bean. When this is the case, beans from different regions will be blended to create the taste the chocolate manufacturer seeks.

Because the flavor of cocoa beans changes from batch to batch and harvest to harvest, most blends and roasts have to be tweaked regularly to achieve exactly the desired flavor, further complicating the blending process.

THE SIGNIFICANCE OF TERROIR FOR COCOA FLAVOR AND QUALITY

You may think it sounds a bit pretentious, in a chocolate context, to use the word *terroir*, a term wine connoisseurs use to indicate that slight variations in growing conditions of grapes can have noticeable effects on the wine produced from those grapes. Taken to its extreme, some wine super-tasters claim to be able to identify the exact location (the terroir) of the vines from which their glass of wine originated—not just the region but, say, the specific hillside. Not many chocolate professionals are quite so exacting, but it's true that where a cacao tree grows has a profound effect on the taste of the beans produced. As with winemaking, major factors in the development of taste are soil and climate, and these are influenced by seasonal variations in weather. The chemical composition of the soil in which the trees grow and the chemical elements in the water affect the taste of the beans. Less obvious influences include elevation, prevailing wind patterns, the amount of rain and when it falls, and the difference in temperature between the hottest and coolest parts of the day and night and season. Weather factors averaged over many years become the climate in which the cacao trees grow, determining the basic flavor profile of the cacao seed.

Seasonal variations in weather affect the flavor of cacao seeds from harvest to harvest. A year that is warmer or cooler than average, or drier or wetter, or with more or less cloud cover and at different times of the day, results in changes in flavor from year to year.

While these seasonal differences have long been celebrated in wine and other gourmet and artisan foods (such as mountain cheeses and fine cured hams), until the early 1990s in chocolate they were to be avoided or masked during manufacture. Consistency of taste in the finished chocolate, regardless of changes in the flavor of the beans used to make the chocolate, was the perfection sought by chocolate manufacturers, chocolatiers, and consumers. After all, who wants to hear that although it was a great harvest in Ocumare the price of chocolate made with beans from the 2007 harvest is five times higher than chocolate made with beans from the 2006 harvest? Or worse news, perhaps, that it was a bad weather year in Ghana so the harvest was down and the chocolate is uninspiring? This may be the norm in the winemaking industry, but as yet very few people think of chocolate in this way. However, a trend toward appreciation of seasonal differences in chocolate was spearheaded in the 1980s by French manufacturers such as Bonnat and Pralus, and the attitude started to spread abroad in 2000.

The Four Main Types of Cacao

FORASTERO

ORIGIN	Amazon River Basin; introduced into Western Africa via the island of Sao Tome.
TREE	Comparatively high yielding and disease resistant
POD	Lower Amazon (Amelonado): yellow pods with smooth outer skin Upper Amazon (UPA): yellow pods with variable shapes Comparatively disease resistant
BEAN	Size: large Interior color: violet
FLAVOR	Robust; not considered to be fine flavor cacao

CRIOLLO

ORIGIN	Central America, Mexico
TREE	Comparatively low yielding and not as resistant to disease
POD	Red, orange, or yellow pods; rough outer skin with longitudinal furrows
BEAN	Size: small to medium Interior color: pale to white (which gave rise to the name Porcelana)
FLAVOR	Delicate and nuanced; considered to be the finest flavor cacao

TRINITARIO

ORIGIN	Island of Trinidad (a natural hybrid between Forastero and Criollo); introduced into Western Africa via the island of Fernando Po (Malabo)
TREE	Intermediate yield and disease resistance between Forastero and Criollo.
POD	Various colors, often purple
BEAN	Size: medium to large Interior color: ranges from violet to pale depending on predominance of Forastero or Criollo strains
FLAVOR	Nuanced to robust; considered to be fine flavor cacao

NACIONAL

ORIGIN	Ecuador, technically considered to be Forastero sub-type exhibiting many Criollo characteristics
TREE	Similar to Trinitario
POD	Similar to Trinitario
BEAN	Size: medium to large Interior color: ranges from violet to pale
FLAVOR	Nuanced to robust; considered to be fine flavor cacao

Once the pods are harvested,
the seeds must be removed
within a matter of a few
hours to a few days.

THE HARVEST

*

HOW CACAO PODS ARE HARVESTED

When harvesting pods, the goal is to cut the stem without damaging the pod, the flower cushion, or the tree. Damaged pods are susceptible to disease, insect damage, and rot, and if the flower cushion is damaged no pods will grow from it ever again. Because of the precision required to cut the stem without damaging either the pod or the flower cushion, harvesting cacao pods is still a manual process.

Ideally, pods that display any visual evidence of disease or insect damage are taken down from the tree, removed from the plantation, and buried or (preferably) burned. However, because farmers get paid by weight, this does not always happen.

HOW CACAO SEEDS ARE REMOVED FROM THE PODS

Once the pods are harvested, the seeds must be removed within a matter of a few hours to a few days. Sometimes the pods are opened and the seeds removed immediately upon harvesting, and sometimes harvested pods are transported to a central site where the seeds are removed. The choice of method usually depends on the availability and organization of available labor.

In general, smallholder farmers will open the pods at their plantations and either perform the post-harvest processing at the plantation or transport just the seeds for post-harvest processing: pods with seeds in them are much bulkier and heavier than seeds alone, and the pods can be left in the fields as compost. On larger plantations and in cooperatives where there are many workers, it often makes sense to transport pods to a central point for opening and post-harvest processing.

CHOCOPHILE FACT

On average cacao trees yield five to six pounds (2.25 to 2.75 kilos) of dried cocoa beans each year.

*

Care must be exercised when opening the pods not to damage the seeds inside. There are two main methods for opening pods. One method uses a machete or other large knife to cut off the top (the stem end) of the pod and then cut a wedge in the flesh that can be levered open to reveal the seeds. The other method uses a blunt mallet to break the flesh of the pod, which is then peeled away to reveal the seeds.

The seeds are arranged within the pod in a pentagonal pattern that's connected to a central internal stem (called the placenta). The placenta must be removed, but the seeds are covered with a very tasty tart-sweet pulp that is left on the seeds for the next step in post-harvest processing.

Ideally, when removing the seeds from the pod, any seeds that might have been damaged when the pods were opened are discarded; these seeds are more vulnerable to attack by mold and mildew that can generate undesirable funky flavors during fermentation and drying. Furthermore, seeds that show any evidence of disease or insect damage should also be discarded. Again, however, because farmers are paid by weight, seeds or beans, no matter their condition, are rarely discarded; this can affect the quality of the chocolate ultimately made from those beans.

How Much Chocolate Is Enough Chocolate? The Future of Cacao Harvesting

The total world harvest of cacao in 2006 was estimated to be about 3 million metric tons (3 million tonnes) or about 1 pound (450 grams) of cocoa beans per person currently living. While this amount meets current global needs, the growing demand for chocolate made with specialty beans and the higher-cocoa-content chocolate esteemed by gourmands means tight supplies and rapidly escalating prices for quality flavor cocoa beans. Luckily, programs around the world are energetically addressing what could become a crisis (or at least a very unhappy situation) for chocophiles. Here's how:

Organization and financing: The fact that smallholder farmers are forming into cooperatives that enable them to pool resources is changing cacao plantation life everywhere. Co-ops can build centralized fermentation and drying facilities that will help them produce better-quality cacao; as a result they can negotiate better finance terms and pricing for their crops.

Education: Most cacao-growing countries are continually engaged in programs to educate farmers about ways to cost-effectively boost production. Much of this effort focuses on plantation management techniques aimed at increasing yield and minimizing loss to diseases and pests.

Disease and pest control: One of the lesser-known facts about cacao is that, even when it isn't certified organic, most of it is de facto organic. Farmers with small holdings are typically too poor to afford pest control of any kind, let alone agricultural chemicals. The methods available to them are labor intensive; many farmers can't afford to do them well, if at all. For example, instead of being removed from the plantation and buried or burned, diseased and damaged pods are simply left on the trees, where they can infect other pods. The International Cocoa Organization estimates that between 25 and 50 percent of the worldwide cacao crop is lost each year because of diseases and pests; in some countries, notably Brazil, which used to be a major exporter of cocoa, the entire cacao economy has been upended.

Cacao hybridization: Tropical agriculture research centers around the world are working to develop cacao hybrids that are high yielding, disease resistant—and taste good, too.

Growing cacao in new regions: One of the best examples is Vietnam, where the government has announced a program to triple the amount of land dedicated to cacao cultivation by 2010. The country's cocoa-planting efforts focus on Forastero and Forastero hybrid beans.

Before the harvest:

1. A cacao nursery in Chiapas, Mexico, near the Guatemalan border. Farmers here are breeding a hybrid they developed through careful selection of desirable tree characteristics over several generations.

2. A mature cacao tree laden with pods, some of which are ready for harvesting.

3. A well-tended cacao farm, the Hacienda la Ceiba, in Venezuela. Note the leaf litter left under the trees (necessary for pollination) and the irrigation ditch.

4. Pods at very different stages of development can be found on a single cacao tree.

5. A cacao pod showing signs of frosty pod rot. The disarming name belies the damage this disease can wreak on a farm.

6. A cacao pod showing signs of blackpod (an infectious disease that causes pods to rot) and insect damage. Affected pods should be removed from the tree and buried or burned. However, on small cacao farms this is rarely done.

Before the harvest

Harvest

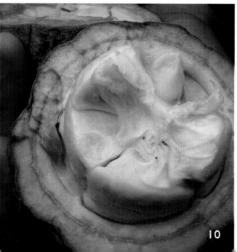

Harvest:

7. A smallholder cacao farmer in Ecuador holding a tool to harvest cacao. A sharp hooked knife is at the end of this long pole, which is used to retrieve pods high overhead.

8. When the pod is near the ground (as is the case here), a machete is used to cut the pod from the tree.

9. Askinosie Chocolate founder Shawn Askinosie using a machete to open a cacao pod. Don't try this at home: the machete is heavy and it would be very easy to lose some fingers.

10. A cacao pod cut in half, showing the pentagonal arrangement of the seeds around the central stem, or placenta.

AFTER THE HARVEST:
FROM FERMENTING THE CACAO TO DRYING THE BEANS
✳

HOW CACAO SEEDS ARE FERMENTED

Once the seeds have been removed from the pods, they must undergo a period of fermentation. Otherwise, the chocolate flavor we know and love cannot fully develop during manufacturing. The length of fermentation is dependent on an incredibly wide range of factors, including the type of seeds being fermented (Forasteros require more fermentation than Criollos; Trinitarios are in-between), the quantity of seeds being fermented, the method of fermentation, and the differential between daytime and nighttime temperatures, to name just a few.

Fermentation can be accomplished by many methods. The time-honored traditional way is to create a "blanket" on the ground with banana leaves, put the seeds into a pile on this blanket, cover the pile with more banana leaves, and then weigh down the leaves with rocks. This method is still widely used today, as the basic materials used to ferment cacao this way are free to the farmer. A modern variation on this method replaces the banana leaves with sheets of plastic, preferably dark, to absorb heat from the sun, and the rocks with cinder blocks.

A variation on this technique involves creating a tent out of black plastic and fermenting the beans underneath. This is usually done on a hard surface such as concrete.

Another method is to put the seeds in fermentation boxes of various methods of construction. (*Box* is used loosely here; often the container is a simple woven basket.) Fermentation boxes have the advantages of keeping the pile of seeds compact and together, stabilizing and controlling temperature, and, if the boxes are arranged in tiers, facilitating the turning of the seeds during fermentation. Box fermentation also makes it possible to handle large quantities of seeds—up to 2,200 pounds (1,000 kilograms) at a time—whereas other methods are limited to much smaller quantities.

Irrespective of the method used, fermentation is a two-part process that takes between three and seven days. The first stage of fermentation is anaerobic, which means it takes place in the absence of air. During this stage, yeasts and microorganisms in the cacao pulp and in the air work on the sugars in the pulp, creating alcohol and generating heat. The heat and the alcohol kill the seeds and keep them from germinating (the germ is very bitter). At the same time, a complex series of chemical reactions is occurring inside the beans, converting complex proteins and complex sugars into simpler chains of amino acids and simpler sugars, while polyphenols are converted into insoluble compounds that oxidize, giving the dry beans their characteristic brown color.

Once a pile of beans has reached a certain temperature and maintained it for a period of time, the pile needs to be turned. In a pile on the ground, the weights and top layer of leaves or plastic are removed, the pile is turned and mixed using a shovel or rake, the beans are piled up again, and the top cover and weights are replaced.

Fermentation boxes are usually designed in sections that come apart to facilitate turning. If the boxes are tiered, the beans spill from a higher position to a lower position at each step of fermentation. Another advantage of this method is more continuous fermentation: new batches start in the upper boxes as batches that are farther along finish in the lower ones.

The second stage of fermentation is aerobic (in the presence of air). Air introduced into the pile during the turning changes the nature of the fermentation process, and the alcohol gets converted to acetic acid (vinegar). More heat is generated, and the complex chemical reactions

The Flavors of Chocolate: Why Fermentation Matters

CCN-51
Nacional varietal + Trinitario
(Criollo + Forastero)

Fermentation has enormous influence on the flavor of the chocolate made with the beans. One prime example of this is CCN-51, a hybrid developed in Ecuador with a lackluster name but other appealing qualities. The CCN-51 is a hybrid of a Nacional varietal with a Trinitario, which itself is a hybrid of Criollo and Forastero cacao. If this explanation is confusing, all you need to know is that the result is a very high-yielding hybrid—trees start bearing harvestable fruit very young and each tree produces a lot of very large pods. Though popular among farmers for this reason, the bean has not been regarded as tasty, which is surprising given the amount of flavor cacao genes in its mix—Nacional *and* Criollo. The reason for this turns out to be simple, in hindsight: CCN-51 hybrids were being fermented as if they were Forasteros; they were being overfermented. Just by changing the fermentation process, the potential for flavor for chocolate made from CCN-51 beans increases dramatically.

that began in the first phase of fermentation continue. The pile is turned once again during the aerobic fermentation stage.

Unfermented beans, used only in very bad chocolate and to make cocoa butter, *never* express the full flavor potential of the genetics of the tree; their complex proteins and sugars have not been broken down into simpler compounds that can be cooked and caramelized during roasting. Under-fermented beans have some of these compounds (and flavors) developed but not all of them. Overfermentation can cause beans to start to rot, introducing flavors of smoked ham, among other off tastes. Other factors, including how long it took the pile to reach the correct temperature, how long it stayed at that temperature, how much oxygen was introduced into the pile during turning, and the differential in temperature between the center of the pile and the edges, influence the amount of fermentation that occurs and therefore the flavor potential of the chocolate made from the beans. As your palate becomes more attuned to the range of flavors in chocolate, you'll begin to recognize the highly appealing flavors and the less-than-desirable off flavors.

HOW COCOA BEANS ARE DRIED

Once the beans have been fermented, they must be dried: wet cocoa beans are susceptible to mold and mildew, and the drying process itself influences the development of the beans' flavor. The best method for drying is "low and slow in the sun." It can take as long as seven days to reduce the moisture level of the bean to the level required—it should be approximately 7 percent water. (If the moisture level is higher, it invites mold and mildew growth during storage and transoceanic shipping. If the moisture level is much lower, the beans become brittle and are very likely to break with handling.)

Often, a concrete patio is used to assist in drying. The beans are laid out on the patio in the morning and as the concrete warms up over the course of the day the beans are raked over to expose wet surfaces to the air. Concrete patios are relatively clean (and easy to clean), and because the concrete absorbs heat during the day, drying on them tends to proceed faster than it does on raised wooden trays. At night, and when rain threatens, the beans are swept up and piled in a dry place until the next day or until the weather clears and the patio dries out.

In some locations, a modified drying process is used with great success. The fermented wet beans are spread out on the drying patio in the morning and then brought back in before the day heats up. This is done to prevent any crusting of the surface of the bean, which slows down the drying process by trapping water and acetic acid inside. The beans are again spread out after the sun passes the zenith and brought back in at dusk. Although the beans are not out in the sun all day, this process can actually speed drying because the drier but not crusty outside acts like a

How cocoa beans are dried: low and slow in the sun.

*

little pump, sucking moisture from the inside of the bean as it rests; this equalizes the water content throughout the bean.

If a drying patio is not available, fermented wet beans are often laid out on the side of the road. This has several disadvantages. The road surface can get too hot, which can slow down the drying process by causing a crust to form on the outside of the beans. While in contact with the asphalt, the fat in the cocoa beans can absorb the tar smell. Finally, if the road is busy, the fat in the beans can absorb the smell of gas and diesel exhaust.

I once had the unfortunate experience of tasting chocolate that was tainted with diesel fumes. Right after I started my business in 1998, I imported some chocolate from France that was trucked from the manufacturer to the port of Le Havre; there it was consolidated on a refrigerated container so I could afford to ship it to the US. Along the way, exhaust fumes leaked into the truck, flavoring the chocolate. I was on vacation when the chocolate was delivered to my office and when I returned I quickly discovered, much to my dismay, that I had about 450 pounds of inedible (and unsellable) chocolate on my hands. That was my first and last venture in the chocolate-importing business!

In many climates it's just not practical to use a drying patio or the side of the road because of rain. Instead, specialized drying sheds are built. The more elaborate of these have pullout trays made from wood and leaves that the beans sit on. The trays are pulled out when it is sunny and then pushed into the shed at night and when it rains. Smaller drying sheds are being used in many South American countries to make it possible for individual farmers to dry their beans on their own land.

It is possible to artificially dry cocoa beans using a fire made from propane (expensive) or coconut husks (free) or other fuels. This is done when the climate is so wet that beans cannot be dried reliably in the sun, even on trays. When drying artificially, a raised bed is constructed with a floor that has perforations that allow warm air to rise through the beans. Done properly, there is nothing wrong with artificially drying beans. However, there are several risks involved that can negatively affect flavor.

One risk of artificial drying is that the beans will get too hot. As can happen when beans are dried on asphalt, a crust forms on the outside of the bean (think of the crust on a piece of toast), slowing down the process considerably; the beans can also get so hot that they burn.

Another risk of artificial drying is that smoke (or other combustion by-products) from the fire will leak out into the drying bed. This is the cause for the smoky flavor found in many beans, especially those from Indonesia, Malaysia, and climatically similar cacao-growing countries. At its best, smoky chocolate (while not exactly desirable) is an interesting flavor and can be used effectively in culinary applications. At its worst, the fat in the beans can absorb the smell of burning hydrocarbons—interesting, yes, but certainly not delectable.

Cocoa-Boom!

After hearing alarming reports that cocoa has been known to explode if it gets hot enough, I did a little research. It seems that cocoa powder *can* spontaneously combust when it reaches a temperature of 329°F (165°C). A dust explosion could also occur if the cocoa powder reaches a density of approximately 40 grams of cocoa powder per cubic meter of air (or about 1.5 ounces of cocoa powder in around 10 cubic feet of air). In other words, unless you plan to put a teaspoon (about 5 grams) of cocoa powder into a convection oven and turn it on "high" (and we strongly advise against this), you don't have to worry about exploding cocoa.

Boom!

After the harvest:

1. In the village of Olboe in Vanuatu, cacao being fermented in the traditional fashion, in a pile of banana leaves.

2. A good-sized box fermentation setup at a small cooperative in Ecuador, Luz y Guia. Fermentation begins in the top row of boxes and at each "turn" cascades into the next lowest set of boxes. At the base of the fermentation setup is a drying patio.

3. Cacao being fermented in small baskets at Hacienda la Ceiba in Venezuela. This method is most often used with small amounts of beans.

4. Cacao being fermented under a tent. Flaps at the end allow easy visual inspection.

5. A worker separating placenta from partially fermented beans before further fermentation.

6. An example of a small drying tent, or *maquesina*, that enables Ecuadorian smallholder cacao farmers to dry their beans even if it's raining.

After the harvest

7. Beans drying in the sun on a concrete drying patio.

8. To protect beans being dried on asphalt, this farmer has laid them down on a cloth.

9. Drying trays in Hawaii, made from wooden frames and corrugated iron, and on legs.

10. A propane burner being used to artificially dry beans in Ecuador. This is an example of a well-built dryer. Often they are jury-rigged from used fifty-gallon drums and other scavenged parts.

11. A worker turning beans to even out the drying process and trying (unsuccessfully) to keep the beans from being burned.

HOW COCOA BEANS ARE GRADED AND SHIPPED

Dried beans are graded according to systems that differ from country to country. Grading depends on the percentage of properly fermented beans, the average weight of beans, and the type and quantity of other defects in the beans. Beans are sampled in lots of one hundred randomly selected beans, which are cut in half (in what is called a "cut test") using a special cocoa-bean guillotine in order to assess their overall quality and the level of any defects such as:

- Slaty cut (indicates no fermentation; refers to color and texture)
- Violet cut (indicates insufficient fermentation; refers to color)
- Brown cut (indicates adequate fermentation; refers to color)
- Molds and mildew
- Insect damage
- Flat and small beans (tend to be difficult to shell)
- Germinated beans
- Unpleasant odors—for example, smoky, hammy (indicates overfermentation)

How Much for Those Beans?

The cut test used to grade cocoa beans, in which the beans are cut in half to look for defects, also takes place during negotiation sessions when chocolate manufacturers buy beans directly from cacao farmers. The results of the cut test, and thus the grade of the beans, will affect the price that the manufacturers will pay for the beans.

Unlike most artisanal foods, virtually all gourmet chocolate is made thousands of miles from where the beans are grown.

Unlike most artisanal foods, which tend to be made near where their ingredients are grown, virtually all gourmet chocolate is made thousands of miles from where the beans are grown. Once beans have been graded, they are put into bags and stored until they are shipped. Shipping almost always takes place via an ocean-going container vessel, and the major challenges are maintaining moisture and humidity levels below the point at which mold and mildew can grow on the beans as well as protecting the beans from insects and rodents.

When the beans arrive in the receiving port, a number of cut tests are again performed on the shipment beans (the number of cut tests performed depends on the size of the shipment); if the beans that arrive in port are substantially different from the beans the buyer contracted to purchase, the buyer has the right to reject the shipment.

Once the beans have been accepted, they are shipped to warehouses in anticipation of what comes next: making chocolate!

MANUFACTURING THE CHOCOLATE

✳

HOW COCOA BEANS ARE CLEANED

The first step in making chocolate is to make sure that the bags of beans being used are free of anything that's not a cocoa bean. Because beans are paid for by weight, it is not unheard of for bags of beans to contain rocks, twigs, nails, and other material. The major issue here is to separate the noncocoa material from the beans so that (a) hard objects don't wreak havoc on the machinery and (b) soft objects such as small twigs and straw don't burn and taint the beans with the smell of smoke. Special machines called, appropriately enough, bean cleaners are used; depending on the quantity of beans to be cleaned, bean cleaners can be very high or amazingly low tech.

Some manufacturers add an extra cleaning step before proceeding to roasting: sanitizing the beans. Sanitizing uses very hot steam to kill any microorganisms that might be left on the outside shell of the cocoa beans. The maximum allowable levels of some of the microorganisms such as ochratoxins (which can cause serious liver damage) are tightly regulated, but some manufacturers take this next step not only in the interest of consumer safety but also because getting the beans slightly wet helps the shell separate from the bean during the next step.

HOW COCOA BEANS ARE ROASTED AND WINNOWED

Once the beans have been cleaned, they are roasted. How long the beans are roasted and at what temperature depends on the type of bean and the type of chocolate being made. In general, longer roasting times at lower temperatures produce better-tasting chocolate than do higher roasting temperatures for shorter periods of time.

The Good, the Bad, and the Bittersweet

The term *bittersweet* when applied to chocolate has no legal definition. According to the FDA, semisweet and bittersweet chocolates are all subcategories of "sweet chocolate," which by law must have at least a 35 percent cocoa content. But there is no agreed-upon point of cocoa content and sugar content at which a semisweet chocolate becomes bittersweet. In fact, the roast of a bean has at least as much to do with the perception of bitterness of a chocolate as the amount of sugar used in the chocolate. The same cocoa bean can be lightly roasted or heavily roasted; which roast is used depends on what the chocolate maker is trying to achieve. Sometimes, over-roasting (and slightly burning) a bean is used to hide the use of inferior-quality beans, as the burnt taste overwhelms virtually all other flavors.

Most unsweetened "baking" chocolate is not manufactured to be eaten by itself but to be used in recipes with other ingredients, especially sugar, flour, and fats. The beans used can be lower quality, over-roasted to compensate for some of the beans' deficiencies, and they don't need to be conched (a complex process that refines the cocoa liquor to make it extremely smooth): the relatively large particle size (larger than 50 microns) won't be evident because flour particles are huge by comparison.

In order to create a 99 or 100 percent chocolate for eating, it is important to select only very-high-quality beans because there are no other ingredients (for example, sugar) that can be used to cover up off flavors. The beans can't be over-roasted, either, because over-roasting increases bitterness.

sweet chocolate
bittersweet
semisweet

After the beans have been roasted and cooled, the beans are cracked (also called kibbling), and then winnowed—the "meat" of the beans is separated from the shells. The shells can be used as mulch (though pets, especially dogs, must be kept from eating the mulch, as the shells contain large amounts of a chemical that can kill them), but often they are simply discarded. The pieces of cocoa bean meat are called *nib* or *nibs*. It is the nibs that are ground to make cocoa liquor, which in turn is used to make chocolate.

Winnowing cocoa beans manually is a tedious and difficult process. The invention of machines that perform this task effectively and efficiently made it possible to make chocolate in very large quantities, and closely follows the development of winnowing machines for other important food crops during the 1800s.

HOW COCOA BEANS ARE GROUND

There are many different ways to make chocolate from cocoa nibs. The method I describe here is one that might be followed by a small-scale or artisanal chocolate maker. Making chocolate on an industrial scale uses techniques and equipment that differ from these significantly.

The first step in converting cocoa nibs into chocolate is grinding the nibs. This takes place in a grinder or melangeur (French for "mixer"). In small-batch production, a melangeur that uses granite millstones is preferable to one that uses stainless steel, which is the material of choice for continuous, nonstop—not small-batch—industrial production.

As the nibs are ground, heat generated from friction causes the fat in the nibs to melt, and as the grinding process continues the size of the cocoa particles becomes smaller and smaller and the resulting paste—which is confusingly called by several names, including cocoa liquor, chocolate liquor, and cocoa mass—becomes thinner and smoother.

The resulting cocoa liquor is pure unsweetened chocolate in its most basic form. Although most cocoa liquor is simply inedible, it is at this point that most major decisions regarding blending are made, as blending is most easily achieved by blending cocoa liquor, not cocoa nibs.

Before the Europeans' arrival in the New World, cocoa liquor was what was used to make the chocolate beverages that were so highly prized. The liquor would have been added to a liquid, often a cold, thin corn gruel, and then spiced using chiles, vanilla, and other locally available spices. The resulting liquid would have been agitated to produce large amounts of froth, which was the most highly valued part of cacao consumption before the Spanish creolized cacao by adding sugar to it and drinking it hot. At this point, the cocoa liquor can be diverted from the chocolate-making process to be separated into cocoa butter and cocoa powder.

HOW COCOA LIQUOR IS REFINED

After the initial grinding, the cocoa liquor needs to be refined. This is because it is difficult to grind the nibs as finely as needed to make the individual particles undiscernible in the mouth. The nibs start out quite large, and the cocoa particles must end up smaller than 20 microns or the finished chocolate will have an unpleasantly gritty texture.

Mechanical refining is one of the key differences between handmade and machine-made chocolate. Using traditional tools such as a metate (a concave stone much like a mortar) and rolling pin, it is simply impossible to grind the cocoa particles small enough so they can't be felt in the mouth. Hand-grinding is even more difficult when white sugar is added, because sugar crystals are very hard to crush.

It is during the refining stage that the milk (if milk chocolate is being made), sugar, and vanilla are added. The cocoa liquor to which these ingredients have been added are fed into the refining machine. Modern refiners resemble printing presses with their multiple steel rollers. Three- and five-roller refiners are the most common. The cocoa liquor is passed through a series of smaller and smaller rollers, which are kept cool to keep the fat in the cocoa liquor from separating out; the smaller rollers therefore turn faster, and the gap between the rollers gets smaller and smaller. What starts out as a thick paste going into the refiner comes out the other end as a dry powder that is ready for the next stage, conching.

HOW COCOA BUTTER AND COCOA POWDER ARE MADE

Cocoa butter is a fat, and cocoa beans contain large amounts of cocoa butter (on average about 50 percent by weight), so cocoa liquor is actually a pretty messy product to make hot beverages with because the fat separates out and floats to the top of the glass. Until the discovery and patenting of a mechanical means to separate cocoa butter from cocoa solids, it was usual in European chocolate houses to use a knife to skim off the cocoa butter that floated to the top of a cup.

Coenraad van Houten is often credited with inventing the cocoa-butter press, but this is not true. There are records of presses that precede his invention. However, van Houten was the first to patent a commercially viable cocoa-butter press. Today there are several different types of cocoa-butter presses in use, including ones that would be recognizable to van Houten.

At its simplest, a cocoa-butter press resembles a cider press. There is a cylinder lined with a fine-mesh sieve to hold the chocolate liquor. Pressure is applied to a piston that fits tightly into the cylinder, and the cocoa butter squeezes through the mesh while the cocoa solids are trapped inside the cylinder. The cocoa butter is usually cleaned to remove any very fine particles of cocoa solids as well as any strong flavors and aromas it might have. This process is called deodorization and involves high-temperature steam and special chemicals.

The cocoa solids are now in the form of a "press cake" that still contains a fair amount of fat, usually 10 to 12 percent or 20 to 22 percent. The press cake is broken up into bits and then ground into cocoa powder. It is possible to make chocolate by recombining the separated cocoa butter and cocoa powder, but usually only relatively low-quality mass-market chocolates are made this way.

Cocoa liquor can also be "dutched," or processed with an alkali. The purpose of dutching is to neutralize or reduce the acidity of the cocoa liquor. (Remember that acetic acid—vinegar—is formed during fermentation, and this acidity is not completely removed during drying, roasting, and grinding.) There are many ways to perform the dutching process. One common method is to add one of several different alkalizing chemicals to the cocoa.

Dutching changes the acidity of the chocolate and therefore its flavor, but other flavor changes may also be noticeable; in particular, dutch-processed cocoa may seem "milder," which is why it is often used to make mass-market chocolate. Dutching also affects the color of the cocoa powder, which is often reddish when unalkalized. At its most extreme, dutching can turn cocoa powder black, which is how Oreo cookies get their characteristic color.

It is also possible to deacidify chocolate liquor without using chemicals; this method is used in industrial chocolate manufacturing, not the manufacture of cocoa butter and powder. Deacidification is accomplished by introducing hot steam into the cocoa liquor. The hot steam causes the volatile aromatic acids (including the vinegary acetic acid) to evaporate very quickly. Deacidifying the chocolate liquor at this stage reduces the amount of time required in the conching stage of production, explained on page 84. However, it is impossible to control which aromatics evaporate when the cocoa liquor is deacidified this way, so the complexity of the flavor of the finished chocolate is compromised.

HOW CHOCOLATE IS CONCHED

Old-style conches resemble large bathtubs that are heated and filled with chocolate; rollers go back and forth from one end of the tub to the other for hours or days at a time, patiently transforming the still-rough product that comes out of the refiner into heavenly elixir. Conching is the final step in the manufacturing process in which the flavor and texture of the finished chocolate can be influenced. During the conching process, several things happen:

1. Additional cocoa butter is added to make the chocolate more fluid and to improve the way it feels as it melts in your mouth.
2. If there are any clumps of cocoa particles (called agglomerates) left in the chocolate, they are broken up into individual particles.
3. Particles that might still be oversize are reduced in size.
4. All of the cocoa particles get covered with fat—either cocoa butter alone or cocoa butter in combination with other fats (for example, the cream in a milk chocolate).
5. Any water and volatile aromatic compounds that remain in the chocolate are evaporated.
6. If lecithin is being used, it is added near the end of conching to further thin out the chocolate, making the molding process easier.

Conching can take as few as four hours or as many as seventy-two.

＊

Conching can take as few as four hours or as many as seventy-two. The longer the conching takes, the more expensive the chocolate will be—and, generally, the more subtle and nuanced the flavors will be. It is possible to over-conche chocolate, which makes it taste flat. Not all small-scale and artisan chocolate manufacturers have separate melangeurs, refiners, and conches. All that machinery is expensive, it takes up a fair amount of space, and transporting the chocolate from one machine to the next introduces a whole different set of problems. In some cases, a single machine called a Universal is used; in other cases, the chocolate maker will have a melangeur and then use a Universal-type machine for refining and conching.

Once the chocolate has finished conching, it needs to be prepared to be molded by a process called tempering. Chocolate hardens not by drying (there is no water in chocolate), but through the process of crystallization of the fats in the cocoa butter. Unlike most other plant fats (and like most animal fats), cocoa butter is solid at room temperature. Because of cocoa butter's unique chemical makeup, there are actually six different configurations of cocoa butter crystals, only one of which (the β_1 form) is stable at room temperature and that delivers a chocolate with a nice snap and sheen. All of the other crystal forms will either start melting around 63°F (17°C), bloom very easily, deliver a chocolate with no snap and no sheen, or some combination of these.

Chocolate is tempered by melting it and raising the temperature above the point where all the cocoa butter crystals are completely melted out. Once all the crystals are melted out, the chocolate is cooled, allowing crystals to form. To force the formation of the proper crystals in the cooling chocolate, chocolate that has already been properly tempered is added to "seed" the formation of the β_1 crystals.

Evaluation:

1. A worker inspects the beans before cutting.

2. A cut test using a purpose-built cutter. This test reveals well-fermented beans with very few defects.

Manufacturing:

3. This roaster at an artisan chocolate company's factory in Tapachula, Mexico, is a handmade contraption built with scavenged parts.

4. Beans are cooled after being roasted.

5. A handmade winnower for small-scale production. Beans are poured in the top, and nibs come out the bottom; the husks are vacuumed away through the tubes at the top.

6. The grinder at an artisan chocolate manufacturer in Mexico.

Evaluation

2

Manufacturing

7. Cocoa beans are ground into liquor in a melangeur.

8. Tasting various cocoa liquors to evaluate the effects of fermentation on flavor.

9. Conching the results of the refining process for smoothness with an old-style concher.

10. After the chocolate is tempered it is molded into bars. This final step yields bars of chocolate.

5

6

9

10

Once the chocolate has been tempered, it gets deposited into molds of various sizes. This is usually done with a machine that portions the chocolate out into the mold cavities. The mold is then vibrated to allow any air bubbles to rise to the surface, and then the mold travels through a cooling tunnel to jump-start the crystallization process. When it emerges from the cooling tunnel, the chocolate may sit to complete the crystallization process before it gets wrapped to protect it from oxygen and moisture.

And there you have it: **a bar of chocolate.**

Making a great chocolate requires a commitment to excellence, attention to detail, and the willingness to do whatever is necessary to maximize the development of chocolate flavor during each step of the chocolate-making process—from harvesting the pods from the cacao tree to molding the chocolate into a bar. In other words, it takes time and money to make great chocolate. •

Cocoa and Cocoa Content: Facts for the Obsessed

- Average weight of one cocoa pod: 380 grams (13 oz)
- Average weight of fresh beans/pod: 100 grams (3.5 oz)
- Average weight of dry beans/pod: 40 grams (1.4 oz)
- 100 kilograms (220 lbs) of fresh beans = 80 kilograms (176 lbs) of fermented beans = 40 kilograms (88 lbs) of dry beans
- One tree produces 3 kilograms (6.6 lbs) of merchantable (dry) cocoa beans each year. One tonne (2,200 lbs) of dry beans comes from 25,000 pods.
- A 250-gram bar of dark chocolate (about 9 oz) requires 3 to 5 pods:
    - 3 pods => 120 grams of dry beans = 105 grams nib = 250-gram bar @ 42% cocoa content
    - 4 pods => 160 grams of dry beans = 140 grams nib = 250-gram bar @ 56% cocoa content
    - 5 pods => 200 grams of dry beans = 175 grams nib = 250-gram bar @ 72% cocoa content

3.

How to Buy Chocolate

(FOR YOURSELF AND OTHERS)

CHOCOLATE IS ONE OF THE MOST AFFORDABLE GOURMET FOODS TO WHICH YOU CAN TREAT YOURSELF. ✳ Yet some people think that gourmet chocolates are way too expensive, needlessly denying themselves one of life's great pleasures. Some people who would not hesitate to pay $75 to $100 for a bottle of wine have a problem paying $10 for a bar of chocolate. You can buy a good cognac for under $30 at your local liquor store but if you want to buy one of France's finest Cognacs you should expect to pay at least $3,000 for a bottle, and an after-dinner glass in any restaurant that carries it will set you back at least $125. Everyday balsamic vinegar in a warehouse store costs about $3.50 a liter, while great seventy-five-year-old AIB-certified balsamic vinegar costs over $165 for a 100-milliliter bottle (approximately ¼ cup), or over $1,600 per liter (about a quart)—*for vinegar*! In other words, the spread between the cost of what you might buy for everyday use and what you buy for special occasions is very high, up to a hundred times more. For wine the price differential is even greater.

Everyday bars of eating and baking chocolate cost between $5 and $10 a pound in the supermarket. The world's most expensive solid eating chocolate is about $100 a pound, and you can purchase a bar of it for $20. That makes the price spread between everyday chocolate and the best and most expensive in the world a small fraction of the spread typical of other gourmet foods.

Imagine that. If you have $20 you can afford to buy the world's most expensive—and maybe the world's best—bar of chocolate. Even the most expensive confections in the world are very affordable (because you can buy them in ones and twos if you want). You can walk into the most exclusive chocolate shop in San Francisco or New York, Paris or Brussels, Barcelona or Turin, and walk away with a completely satisfying chocolate experience for less than the price of an *aucourantini* in a New York nightclub.

One of the other great things about chocolate is that good reviews of chocolate don't raise the price through the stratosphere. With wine, a coveted 95+ rating means that the price usually increases overnight, often tripling in value, especially for reds that can be cellared and that will improve with age. Because chocolate does not age gracefully over many years the way wines can, and because there is no collectors' market for chocolate as there is with wine, ratings have virtually no impact on the price you pay for the chocolate you love.

Part of the fun of being a chocophile is in placing the value of the experience of eating a good chocolate in its proper perspective with respect to cost. As you learn more about chocolate and how to discern, understand, and appreciate its subtle nuances, you'll come to realize that you deserve to treat yourself to the best you can buy—and that you can do it for less than what you're currently spending for your afternoon grande half-caf no-foam soymilk latte.

HOW **NOT** TO BUY CHOCOLATE

✳

MISTAKE #1 BUYING CHOCOLATE BASED SOLELY ON WHERE IT IS MADE.
This is sort of like saying that French wine is the best just because it is made in France. The reality is a lot more complex than that, and, just as it is now possible to buy great wines made in every part of the world, it is possible to buy some pretty lousy wines made in France. Ultimately, it all comes down to what you like to drink. The same thing is true with chocolate: it's not better just because it's made in Belgium. Sure, there's a lot of high-quality chocolate made in Belgium, but there's a fair amount of ordinary chocolate made there, too—and a lot of great chocolate that's made elsewhere.

MISTAKE #2 BUYING CHOCOLATE BASED SOLELY ON ITS COCOA CONTENT.
Buying chocolate based on cocoa percentage is a lot like buying vodka based on alcohol content. To suggest that an 86-proof vodka is better than an 80-proof vodka just because it has a 3 percent higher alcohol content is absurd. The same thing is true for chocolate: a chocolate with 70 percent cocoa content is not inherently better than a chocolate with 68 percent cocoa content.

Despite all the marketing hype that tries to convince you otherwise, there is absolutely no relationship between cocoa content and chocolate quality. None. Zip. Nada.

How Cocoa Content Is Calculated

Cocoa content refers to the total amount of cocoa—cocoa solids plus cocoa butter—in a chocolate. It is the combination of the amount of cocoa liquor and any added cocoa butter.

"Cocoa content" and "cocoa solids content" are not the same thing, however. A bar with 70 percent cocoa solids content would almost certainly be inedible.

There is also no relationship between cocoa content and whether or not a chocolate is considered semisweet or bittersweet; both are technically "sweet chocolate," but neither is defined more precisely than that. Sweetness depends on the quantity of sugar in a chocolate, and over-roasting is a primary contributor to bitterness in a chocolate.

MISTAKE #3 BUYING CHOCOLATE IN THE WRONG PLACE.

When you want to buy great wine, you go to a specialty wine store. When you want to buy great cheese, olive oil, or balsamic vinegar, you go to a specialty food store. You could go to the supermarket to buy these things, but you won't have access to the same quality selection. The same thing is true with chocolate. If you want great chocolate, go to a store that specializes in selling chocolate. In addition to having a larger selection and knowledgeable help, a specialty store will almost certainly sell fresher chocolate than anything you can buy in the supermarket.

MISTAKE #4 BUYING CHOCOLATE THAT IS NOT STRICTLY FRESH.

The best chocolates—plain bars as well as confections—are the ones that were made in the last twenty-four hours. While the shelf life of a hand-made artisan chocolate might be measured in weeks, there is no doubt that it is at its best within hours or days of being made.

Everyone knows that the fresher the fish, the better it is. You can buy good frozen fish, but something happens during the freezing and thawing process, and it's still not the same as fresh. The same holds true for chocolate. It is possible to freeze chocolate—and it often is frozen for shipment and storage—but, as with fish, no matter how good it is when it's thawed, it's still not the same. European chocolate brands tend to taste better in Europe than they do in the United States, even if the company says that they are flown in overnight: they are fresher when you eat them close to where they were made. (Another reason European chocolates taste better in Europe is because you're eating them in Europe.)

CHOCOPHILE FACT
You can't eat the box that the chocolates come in, so don't be seduced by fancy packaging.

*

MISTAKE #5 BUYING CHOCOLATE THAT CONTAINS NON–COCOA BUTTER FATS.
"Real" chocolate, to borrow a phase from Chantal Coady, a British chocolatier, contains no fat other than cocoa butter. In the European Union, manufacturers are allowed to replace (substitute) up to 5 percent of the cocoa butter with alternative vegetable fats that are called "cocoa-butter equivalents" and "cocoa-butter replacements." This is done to reduce the cost of making the chocolate, at the expense of chocolate quality. Here in the United States, manufacturers are allowed to add dairy ingredients (such as butter oil, milk fat, or whey) into sweet chocolate (a category that includes what we refer to as "dark chocolate"). When you can, stay away from chocolates that contain non–cocoa butter fats.

When looking at the ingredients in chocolate confections, you need to take into account the fats that might be used in the fillings or centers: dairy fats are acceptable if they're used in the fillings (some caramels, for example, would be impossible to produce without cream). Nondairy fats, however, simply reduce the cost of manufacturing and at the same time act as preservatives, which means that the confection might not be at its freshest when you buy it. In any case, try to avoid buying anything that includes partially hydrogenated oils, especially tropical oils such as coconut oil or palm kernel oil, as these are the least heart-healthy of all fats. For other things to look for when reading the label on a bar of chocolate, see page 102.

MISTAKE #6 BUYING CHOCOLATE BASED ON ITS PRICE TAG.
Great chocolate ain't cheap, but very good chocolate can be had remarkably inexpensively if you pay attention to price but don't let it be your sole guide.

The chocolate industry breaks down into four segments based on price. Following are the price categories and examples of commonly seen brands that fall into each category:

- *Mass market* (for example, Russell Stover or Whitman's): less than $15 per pound, or about $33 per kilogram;
- *Mass-market premium* (for example, See's or Fannie May): $15 to $25 per pound, or about $33 to $55 per kilogram;
- *Gourmet* (for example, Lake Champlain Chocolates or Godiva Gold): $25 to $40 per pound, or about $55 to $88 per kilogram;
- *Prestige* (for example, La Maison du Chocolat or Godiva G): over $40 per pound, or about $88 per kilogram.

Consider buying chocolate based on the price per piece, not the price per pound.

The price per piece depends entirely on the chocolatiers, the cost of the chocolate and the other ingredients they are using, the market they are trying to sell their product to (for example, gourmet or prestige), and the size of the pieces they produce. Pieces produced in Europe or in a European style tend to be smaller—½ ounce (14 grams) or less—and are therefore less expensive per piece, even though the price per pound might be quite high.

Pieces produced in the United States or in the American style tend to be much larger, often weighing in at a full ounce (28 grams) or more; even though the price per pound may be in the middle of the gourmet range, the price per piece is quite high. Thinking this way leads you to value the piece, not the price. When you want to eat two pieces of chocolate, you can decide how much those two pieces will cost you. I was startled one day when I went to La Maison du Chocolat in New York and ordered a selection of chocolates for myself and a friend. Although La Maison is widely considered to be one of the best chocolatiers in the world and the price is at least $70 per pound, I ended up buying two each of five different chocolates for about $10, which I thought was very reasonable.

Mass

Market

∗

Mass

Market

Premium

∗

Gourmet

∗

Prestige

A FIELD GUIDE TO TOP CHOCOLATE BRANDS

Large-Scale Industrial Chocolate Manufacturers

A large-scale industrial chocolate manufacturer is capable of making tonnes of chocolate per day; in fact, over 15,000 tonnes (33,069,339 pounds) of chocolate of all kinds is made every day worldwide. Following are the names of many large-scale chocolate manufacturers and brands that are available in local supermarkets, specialty stores, and online.

This list is not comprehensive and does not include companies that specialize in producing chocolate that is generally available only to other chocolate and candy companies or to professionals and not the general public.

Archer Daniels Midland (US):
www.admworld.com
Ambrosia, Merckens

Barry Callebaut (Switzerland):
www.barry-callebaut.com
Callebaut, Carma, Cacao Barry, Van Leer

Belcolade (Belgium): www.belcolade.com

Cadbury Schweppes (UK): www.cadbury.co.uk
Green & Black's: www.greenandblacks.com

Cargill (US): www.cargillfoods.com
Gerkens; Wilbur: www.wilburchocolate.com

Chocovic (Spain): www.chocovic.es

El Rey (Venezuela): www.elreychocolate.com

Felchlin (Switzerland): www.felchlin.com

Frey (Switzerland): www.chocolat-frey.com

Guittard (US): www.guittard.com

Hershey's (US): www.hersheys.com
Dagoba: www.dagobachocolate.com;
Scharffen Berger: www.scharffenberger.com

Kraft (US): www.kraft.com

Lindt (Switzerland): www.lindtusa.com
Ghirardelli (US): www.ghirardelli.com

Masterfoods/Mars (US): www.masterfoods.com
Dove: www.dovechocolate.com

Michel Cluizel (France):
www.chocolatmichelcluizel.com

Nacional de Chocolates (Colombia):
www.chocolates.com.co
Chocolates Santander:
www.chocolatesantander.com

Nestlé (Switzerland): www.nestle.ch

Schokinag (Germany): www.schokinag.com

Valrhona (France): www.valrhona.com

World's Finest Chocolate (US):
www.worldsfinestchocolate.com

Artisan Chocolate Manufacturers

I spent a long time trying to figure out how to define "artisan" when it came to the manufacture of chocolate, and to my mind there is no distinct point when an artisan chocolate maker's business grows and is no longer artisan. Traditionally, the word artisan connotes "handcrafted," but in order to make quality chocolate it is necessary to use machinery in each and every step of the manufacturing process. Another connotation of artisan is the clear presence of a person's hand in the finished product. For many products and artisan foods, this usually reveals itself as small variations in the finished product due to the materials being used and the very nature of handcrafting, and I think that this idea is useful in determining what makes a chocolate manufacturer "artisan."

Certainly, one important aspect of artisan chocolate manufacturing is small-batch production, typically no more than one tonne at a time and often much smaller. It is harder to control the consistency that is a hallmark of industrial products in batch production, so perhaps another aspect of artisan chocolate making is not only a willingness to accept differences among batches but an embrace of the liberating possibilities those differences open up.

Following are the names of some artisan chocolate manufacturers.

Amano Chocolate (US):
    www.amanochocolate.com
Amedei (Italy): www.amedei.it
Askinosie Chocolate (US): www.askinosie.com
Bernachon (France): www.bernachon.com
Blanxart (Spain): www.blanxart.com
Bonnat Chocolatier (France):
    www.bonnat-chocolatier.com
Domori (Italy): www.domori.com
Haigh's (Australia): www.haighschocolates.com.au
Jacques Torres (US): www.mrchocolate.com

Original Hawaiian Chocolate Factory (US):
    www.originalhawaiianchocolatefactory.com
Plantations (US/Ecuador): www.echocolates.com
Pralus (France): www.chocolats-pralus.com
Richart (France): www.richart-chocolates.com
Scharffen Berger Chocolate Maker (US):
    www.scharffenberger.com
Slitti (Italy): www.slitti.it
Soma Chocolatemaker (Canada):
    www.somachocolate.com
Theo Chocolate (US): www.theochocolate.com

If you are surprised at some of the names that might be missing from this list, note that there are many producers of chocolate bars in the world that do not manufacture their own chocolate—Chocolove (www.chocolove.com), Dagoba (www.dagobachocolate.com), and Nōka (www.nokachocolate.com) are examples. Instead, they purchase chocolate in bulk, usually but not always made to their specifications, and flavor, mold, package, and market finished bars.

Places to Order Chocolate Online

Criteria for inclusion in this list include the quality and diversity of the chocolates on offer.

Chocolate.com

The Chocolate.com website has one of the largest truffle selections available online, but offers bars from only a very small number of companies. The website does not actually warehouse most of the products it sells (if it warehouses any); instead, when an order is placed on the website the company in turn places an order with the chocolate maker and the product gets drop-shipped from the maker or importer. This ensures the freshness of the chocolate, as it is not sitting around in a warehouse for any length of time. The website is headquartered in the Boston, Massachusetts, area.

ChocolateSource.com

In addition to its own brand, Nirvana, ChocolateSource specializes in chocolates from Belgium while also offering products from France, Germany, Venezuela, and the United States. ChocolateSource offers a range of eating and baking chocolates, truffles, and specialty and gifting items. It is located in Wellesley, Massachusetts.

ChocolateTradingCo.com

A good source for quality chocolate if you live in the UK or the EU.

Chocosphere.com

Featuring products from more than thirty-five manufacturers, Chocosphere offers one of the largest selections of chocolates for chocophiles of every taste. Chocosphere sells eating and baking chocolates, truffles, and specialty items. Chocosphere is located in Portland, Oregon.

DiscoverChocolate.com

Edited and published by this book's author, Discover Chocolate specializes in hard-to-find chocolates (mostly solid chocolates for eating and baking) as well as specialty tasting selections that simply can't be found anyplace else. Many tasting selections come with tasting notes and ratings sheets based on the techniques and rating system developed for this book. Discover Chocolate's warehouse is located in Larchmont, New York.

SeventyPercent.com

"Seventy percent" refers to the cocoa content of a chocolate, and Seventy-Percent's mission is to rate, review, and sell quality chocolate.

The relationship you want to have with your chocolatier is the relationship your grandmother wanted to have with her butcher.

HOW TO READ THE INGREDIENTS LABEL
OF A BAR OF CHOCOLATE

✳

As with other foods, manufacturers are required to list the ingredients they put into their chocolate and chocolate confections. Reading the ingredients label can tell you a lot about a chocolate and why it tastes a particular way. As with other foods, manufacturers are required to list ingredients from highest percentage to lowest percentage.

"DARK CHOCOLATE" BARS

People who are truly serious about chocolate make sure that the first ingredient that is listed is cocoa, which can also be called cocoa liquor, chocolate liquor, or cocoa mass. In most cases, the second ingredient listed will be sugar. For the best, cleanest taste, manufacturers use refined white cane sugar. Other sugars or sweeteners can impart an unusual texture or flavor to the chocolate. Unrefined cane syrup, for example, can impart flavors of molasses to a chocolate. This is not necessarily bad, but you should be aware of where the flavor comes from.

Dark chocolate (cocoa content 70% min.)

INGREDIENTS
chocolate liquor, sugar, **cocoa butter**, natural vanilla flavor

The third ingredient most often listed will be cocoa butter. Cocoa butter is added during conching to thin the chocolate and improve the way it melts in your mouth. The combined total of the cocoa and any added cocoa butter comprises the cocoa content of the bar. Chocolate can also contain small amounts of lecithin and vanilla, which are discussed on page 106.

If the first ingredient in a bar of "dark chocolate" is sugar, you can expect the chocolate to be sweeter than a chocolate that lists cocoa as the first ingredient. Which one should you call bittersweet and which one semi-sweet? That depends as much on how the beans are roasted as on how much sugar there is in the chocolate.

Why Is "Dark Chocolate" in Quotes?

According to the U.S. Food and Drug Administration, there's no such thing as dark chocolate. What we commonly refer to as dark chocolate actually falls under the heading "sweet chocolate" in the regulations that define the minimum cocoa content (and other ingredients) in what is called semi-sweet and bittersweet chocolates. Unknown to most people, the acceptable list of ingredients in sweet chocolate includes dairy ingredients such as butter oil, milk fat, and whey.

Most people believe that dark chocolate is any chocolate that does not have milk in it. And, while none of the dairy ingredients above are exactly milk, they are all derived from milk. Even unsweetened baking chocolate can have these dairy ingredients in them. Butter oil, milk fat, and whey, however, often change the texture of the chocolate: most commonly they contribute to a "pasty" texture in the mouth that lingers unappetizingly. It is highly unlikely that the chocolate industry will lobby the FDA to add a special category (officially called a "standard of identity") for dark chocolate, even though they lobbied for years to get the FDA to approve a standard of identity for white chocolate, and even though the change would be fairly simple: dark chocolate should contain no dairy ingredients. Major chocolate manufacturers use dairy products in "dark" chocolate not to pull the wool over anyone's eyes, but because dairy products help stabilize the fat in the chocolate and lengthen its shelf life without the need to add other preservatives. For now it's up to you to read the label to figure out if there are any dairy ingredients in a "dark" chocolate.

Think of the taste of a cup of black espresso. It's bitter because the beans are heavily roasted. If you add sugar, it's bitter *and* sweet. It's possible to make an espresso-style beverage using beans that are roasted less heavily; it will be less bitter, and if you add the same amount of sugar it will seem sweeter than espresso made with espresso beans. This balancing of bitter and sweet flavors is part of what chocolate manufacturers do when making and blending chocolate, but there are no clear guidelines that spell out what a semisweet chocolate is and what a bittersweet chocolate is. It's up to you to decide, or ignore the distinction altogether.

dark
vs.
milk

YES, VIRGINIA, THERE IS SUCH A THING
AS GOOD MILK CHOCOLATE

*

Milk chocolate is the white Zinfandel of the chocolate world; it doesn't get the respect it deserves. For many people, chocolate is dark or it's not really chocolate, and the line is not often crossed willingly. Dark-chocolate lovers see themselves as being superior to milk-chocolate lovers, and milk-chocolate lovers are continually apologizing for liking milk chocolate. (Dark- and milk-chocolate lovers find common ground in heaping scorn on those who prefer white chocolate.) What you like is what you like, and there's no reason to feel superior if you like dark chocolate or apologetic if you like milk chocolate.

I happen to like good milk chocolate but in my experience there are far fewer really good milk chocolates than there are really good dark chocolates. There is even at least one white chocolate worth eating—"Icoa" from El Rey, because it is made with undeodorized cocoa butter and has a mild chocolate flavor.

> **Milk chocolate (cocoa content 62% min.)**
>
> **INGREDIENTS** cocoa, cocoa butter, milk powder, cane sugar

There is increasing interest in something called "dark milk chocolate"—milk chocolate with a cocoa content of at least 45 percent. (Some dark milk chocolates boast cocoa contents of more than 70 percent.) What makes dark milk chocolate interesting is that it combines the intense chocolate flavor of a high-cocoa-content dark chocolate with some of the creaminess and mouthfeel normally associated with milk chocolate. Dark milks also tend to be less sweet than sweet chocolates of the same percentage, because much of the sugar is replaced with milk or cream.

THE SKINNY ON LECITHIN AND VANILLA IN CHOCOLATE

✳

Neither lecithin nor vanilla is required to make high-quality chocolate. In fact, both are often added as shortcuts, as ways to make it easier and less expensive to manufacture chocolate.

Lecithin, usually derived from soybean oil, is an emulsifier, a substance that helps two other substances that don't want to mix, mix. Think of oil and vinegar: they don't mix. If you add some mustard, however, and give it a good shake, the ingredients in the mustard will mix with the oil and vinegar to make the emulsion we call a vinaigrette. The emulsion is usually not very stable, and if you let it sit for a while it will separate.

Chocolate is an emulsion too, one in which cocoa-powder particles are suspended in fat—cocoa butter. In order to be stable, the cocoa butter must crystallize in the correct way. In order to be smooth and creamy and not taste gritty, the cocoa-powder particles must be completely coated with fat. Making sure that the cocoa particles are covered with cocoa butter happens during the conching process. Before lecithin was used, cocoa butter was added to thin the chocolate out. Lecithin makes it possible to use less cocoa butter (making chocolate cheaper to manufacture), and it does a good job of helping make sure that the cocoa particles are covered with fat, which reduces conching time (also reducing costs).

Vanilla, derived from the pods of a variety of orchid, is one of the spices found in the New World that has been used to flavor cacao for thousands of years. Vanilla is a very distinct and identifiable flavor, but it is also a very powerful one that must be used judiciously. In chocolate making, vanilla is used in one of several ways:

- Like salt, as way to enhance the flavor of the chocolate;
- In small amounts to cover up minor differences in the flavor of blended chocolates due to inconsistencies in the flavors of the raw ingredients; or
- In large amounts to mask major differences in chocolate flavor due to major blend inconsistencies or the use of low-quality beans.

In and of itself, the use of vanilla in chocolate is not bad. When it is used, it should be in the form of real vanilla ("natural vanilla") instead of vanilla extract. The artificial form of vanilla, called ethyl vanillin, leaves a distinct chemical flavor in the mouth, and for that reason chocolates containing it should be avoided whenever possible.

INGREDIENTS
sugar, chocolate liquor, cocoa butter, cream powder, non fat milk powder, soy lecithin—an emulsifier, natural vanilla flavor

May contain egg, wheat, tree nuts, and peanuts.

Lecithin? Take It or Leave It

Increasingly, chocolate manufacturers interested in quality are eliminating lecithin from their chocolates. In most cases this is because lecithin is primarily derived from soybeans, and most soybeans grown in the world have been genetically modified. Companies interested in making GMO-free chocolate are faced with trying to find cost-equivalent supplies of GMO-free lecithin or simply doing without, and many are opting to do without.

SHELF LIFE AND PROPER STORAGE OF CHOCOLATE

※

The main enemies of chocolate and chocolate confections are temperature, oxygen, and humidity.

TEMPERATURE

When storing chocolate, avoid subjecting it to rapid changes in temperature. If the chocolate gets too warm and then cools quickly it can lose temper, which means that the cocoa butter crystals align in unwanted patterns, making the chocolate less stable. Cocoa butter bloom can form, and the chocolate will become unsightly. If the chocolate is too cold and then warms up quickly, moisture in the air can condense on the chocolate, causing sugar bloom to form and ruining the texture of the chocolate permanently.

Does Chocolate Improve with Age?

Not in the same way that many wines, especially red wines, do. If chocolate did improve with age you'd see the same interest in chocolate origins and vintages as you do in wines, and chocolate made in "good years" would cost more than chocolate made in "bad years"—and that is clearly not the case.

Some people do believe that chocolate continues to get better the longer it sits; they advocate taking large bars of couverture (chocolate with a higher percentage of cocoa butter often used to cover chocolate confections) and setting them aside for years. I've never done this, I don't know anyone who has, and I don't know anyone who recommends it. The cocoa butter in chocolate continues to slowly crystallize, so I imagine the texture would eventually change to something that is crunchy, dry, and inedible. If you want to try aging chocolate at home, wrap the bar very well to make sure that no moisture can get in and make sure to put it some place where the temperature doesn't vary much from about 50°F (10°C)—ever. Leave the bar alone for at least a couple of years (yeah, right). Let me know how it turns out . (You can contact me at the email address in the introduction.)

Chocolate bars should be stored between 60°F (16°C) and 68°F (20°C). At this temperature, dark chocolate bars can still taste perfectly good after two years, and milk chocolate bars after one year. Chocolate confections can be stored at this temperature and last as long as the manufacturer's "best by" or "consume before" recommendation on the box. It is possible to extend the shelf life of the chocolates slightly by bringing the chocolates to a lower temperature, as long as proper precautions are taken—these are laid out on page 110, in "Refrigerating and Freezing Techniques."

OXYGEN

Oxygen is a highly active gas. Its effect on chocolate bars is not all that noticeable unless the wrapping of the chocolate is punctured or torn somehow. If this happens, over time the chocolate will start to taste stale and take on the flavors of strong smells in its vicinity, and the texture can become very brittle, dry, and sandy.

With chocolate confections, oxygen acts as a catalyst that causes any dairy ingredients in the centers to go bad (they literally turn to cheese). Much of the work to protect chocolate from this is done by the chocolatier—a thick shell of chocolate, for example, can act as an air-tight barrier, making it harder for oxygen to affect the dairy ingredients in a ganache—at the expense of the delicacy of the confection. Chocolatiers can add preservative ingredients to the centers, or they can reduce the amount of dairy in the ganache. Reducing the amount of dairy results in a drier, denser filling, which can be partially compensated for with the addition of an "invert" form of sugar, such as sorbitol, which acts as a preservative while adding a sensation of moisture. A less intrusive technique is to mix the ganache in a vacuum to reduce the effects of spoilage due to oxygen. Some chocolatiers vacuum-seal their chocolates in plastic film and remove oxygen from the box, replacing it with an inert gas such as nitrogen to extend the shelf life of their products without using preservatives.

°F (C)

*

O_2

*

H_2O

Humidity becomes a problem only when it is extreme. Very low humidity can cause the chocolate to "dry out," and the texture can become brittle, dry, and sandy.

High humidity is a problem during rapid changes in temperature. Moisture condensing on the chocolate can pull some of the sugar out of the chocolate to the surface, completely ruining its texture.

REFRIGERATING AND FREEZING TECHNIQUES

The best thing to do is to buy chocolate fresh, in quantities sufficient only for your immediate needs, but this is not always possible. If you buy or are given a large amount of chocolate—either bars or confections—that you won't be able to consume right away, here are the steps you should take to refrigerate, freeze, and thaw it successfully. Keep in mind, however, that milk or dark chocolate bars can be kept at 50 to 60°F (10 to 16°C) for at least a year, so if you have a consistently cool spot in your house you can store chocolate there instead of refrigerating it or freezing it.

1. Divide the chocolate into individual serving portions. Opening up a bag of frozen chocolate to extract one or two pieces is a sure way to ruin the rest of it.
2. Wrap each serving in a press-and-seal-type plastic wrap.
3. Place each serving portion into a small plastic freezer-weight zipper-lock bag with a piece of paper towel, extracting as much air as possible when closing the zipper. Make sure to label the bag with the type of chocolate and the date.
4. Place the plastic bag in the refrigerator.
5. Check the bag after fifteen minutes: if any moisture has condensed on the inside of the plastic bag, replace the paper towel with a fresh one. Check again every fifteen minutes until there is no more moisture in the bag.

6. When the chocolate is cool, place the sealed individual portions into a larger freezer-weight zipper-lock bag.

At this point, you can leave the chocolate in the refrigerator if you like. However, take care to keep the chocolate away from the coldest parts of the fridge, where it might freeze.

7. If you do want to freeze the chocolate, place the large zipper-lock bag in the freezer.

To thaw the frozen chocolate, reverse the procedure:

1. Take the desired amount of chocolate out of the large freezer-weight zipper-lock bag, making sure to remove as much air as possible from the bag when you re-close it and making sure that the zipper is completely closed.
2. Put the chocolate you took from the freezer into the refrigerator. After thirty minutes or so, check the bag to see if any moisture has condensed on the inside. If it has, place a paper towel in the bag and re-close it securely. Let the chocolate thaw in the refrigerator for at least eight hours.
3. After the chocolate has thawed, remove it and allow the chocolate to come to room temperature while still in the bag. Keep the chocolate away from sources of heat and out of direct sunlight. A cupboard is a good place to let the chocolate warm to room temperature.
4. Remove the chocolate from the bag, arrange it on a plate, and enjoy!

THE PERFECT PLACE TO STORE CHOCOLATE

A humidity-controlled wine cellar is the perfect place to store chocolate. Store your bars at red-wine temperature and your confections at white-wine temperature. Make sure to allow the chocolates to warm to room temperature before eating them, and take care if the humidity in the room is a great deal higher than in the cellar so that moisture does not condense on the chocolate. (Although it can take several days for bloom to appear, "sweating" chocolate does not look very nice.) If there is a large humidity differential, simply lay paper towels over the chocolate to absorb some of the excess moisture when you take the chocolate out of the wine cellar.

The Best Chocolate Shop in the World?

L'Etoile d'Or
30, rue Fontaine
Paris

When I visit a new city, my first stop is almost always a local chocolate shop. If you're ever in Paris, be sure to visit L'Etoile d'Or, located not far from the Place Blanche metro stop and down the street from the Moulin Rouge. Denise Acabo's den of delectability offers products from the finest names in France—often those that can't be bought anywhere else: Bernachon, Le Roux, and Dufoux are just three. You can also find better-known brands like Bonnat, Cluizel, and Valrhona, but Mme Acabo very carefully selects only those that meet her demanding standards. If you are not fluent in French, bring along a translator or guide, as Mme Acabo's command of English does not come close to her understanding of chocolate.

HOW TO BUY HANDMADE AND ARTISAN CHOCOLATES

✳

Although every chocolate connoisseur has his or her own criteria, in my opinion, there are two major traits that distinguish great chocolatiers from merely good ones:

• Consistently successful taste combinations; and
• Consistently high-quality production standards.

Good chocolatiers offer many delicious pieces in which the flavors are harmonious and in balance, but they also have a few pieces that leave you wondering what they were thinking when they dreamed up those particular combinations. A great chocolatier, on the other hand, only offers pieces in which the flavor combinations work: any combination that is not up to standards is rejected, or the recipe is reworked until it's indisputably perfect.

One of the greatest challenges facing a chocolatier is production consistency. It's very hard to make thousands of the same pieces over and over, each a perfect work of culinary art, each reflecting the chocolatier's enthusiasm for her craft as if it were the first chocolate she ever made. Great chocolatiers rise to the challenge of maintaining quality and artistry in their often very repetitive work, day after day, year after year. A truly great chocolatier should be able to deliver divine confections any day of the year.

Many people say that one way to tell the quality of a company's ice cream is to taste the vanilla. If the vanilla ice cream is good, then chances are that the company's other flavors will also be good. When you want to know how good chocolatiers are, pick the simplest pieces and evaluate those. If chocolatiers can make really good plain ganaches and caramels, for example, their other pieces will probably be about the same quality.

Start by asking your chocolatier, "What's good today?"

HOW TO BUY A GREAT BOX OF CHOCOLATES
(AND KNOW WHAT YOU'RE GETTING)

※

The relationship you want to have with your chocolatier is the relationship your grandmother wanted to have with her butcher. Over time, your butcher got to know your grandmother, and your grandmother could walk into the shop and ask, "What's good today?" The butcher, because he knew what was fresh and what your grandmother's likes and dislikes were, repaid her loyalty and made recommendations that she could trust.

Nowadays it's much harder to develop those relationships, but it's always worth the effort: your loyalty will be repaid with access to inside information about what's freshest and best. In the absence of that relationship, however, here's what you should do when you're in a shop buying handmade or artisan chocolates you've never tasted before:

- Ask what's freshest. There is a direct relationship between freshness and quality. Chocolates that were made yesterday are simply going to taste better than those that have been frozen or that have been sitting in a display case for weeks (or in a warehouse for months).
- Tell your server what you like and ask him or her what pieces come closest.
- Ask your server what the shop's most popular pieces are. In addition to being popular, the high turnover probably also means that those pieces will be the freshest.
- Ask your server what his or her favorite pieces are. In most cases, the person behind the counter will have tasted everything and can make recommendations. You can then ask questions about the sweetness, flavor, and texture of the pieces that sound interesting to you.
- If you are still undecided, ask which pieces the chocolatier is proudest to be offering. Try those.

A FIELD GUIDE TO TOP CHOCOLATIERS

There are literally thousands of chocolatiers in the United States, and thousands more in the rest of the world. The list that follows, while not comprehensive, of course (chocolate shops, like other business enterprises, tend to come and go) represents chocolates I have personally tasted and/or reviewed and rated. It is organized by the price categories provided in the Chocophile.com rating system. Within each price category, companies are ordered alphabetically, and in order to be included in this list they must have received a minimum of a "Good" rating.

Many companies fit into more than one category, but, with only a few exceptions, they are listed only in the category that the company markets itself to. Following the name of the company and its headquarters city is the style of the chocolate according to the Chocophile.com rating system. Virtually all of the companies mentioned here make their products available online as well as through at least one company-owned retail outlet, and often sell through other channels such as third-party catalogs.

PRESTIGE

Amedei (Pisa, Italy) Belgian: www.amedei.it

Anna Shea Chocolates (Tarrytown, NY) Belgian: www.annasheachocolates.com

Bernachon (Lyon, France) French: www.bernachon.com

Bernard Castelain (Avignon, France) French: www.chocolat-castelain.com

Bonnat Chocolatier (Voiron, France) French: www.bonnat-chocolatier.com

Byrne & Carlson (Portsmouth, NH) French: www.byrneandcarlson.com

Castelanne (Nantes, France) French: www.castelanne.com

Charlemagne (Herstal, Belgium) Belgian: www.charlemagne.be

Chocolat Moderne (New York, NY) Belgian: www.chocolatmoderne.com

Christian Constant (Paris, France) French: www.christianconstant.com

Christopher Elbow (Kansas City, MO) Nouvelle American: www.elbowchocolates.com

Christopher Norman Chocolate (New York, NY) Nouvelle American: www.christophernorman-chocolates.com

Chuao Chocolatier (Encinitas, CA) Nouvelle American: www.chuaochocolatier.com

The Cocoa Tree (Franklin, TN) Nouvelle American: www.thecocoatree.com

Coppeneur (Bad Honneg, Germany) Belgian: www.coppeneur.com

DC Duby Wild Sweets (Vancouver, BC) Nouvelle American: www.dcduby.com

Donnelley Chocolates (Santa Cruz, CA) French: www.donnellychocolates.com

Fran's Chocolates (Seattle, WA) Belgian: www.franschocolates.com

Godiva Chocolatier (G, Platinum—New York, NY) Belgian: www.godiva.com

Intemperantia (Pacific Palisades, CA) Belgian:
www.intemperantia.com

Jacques Torres (New York, NY) Belgian:
www.mrchocolate.com

Jean-Paul Hévin (Paris, France) French:
www.jphevin.com

Joel Durand (San Remy de Provence, France)
French: www.chocolat-durand.com

Kee's Chocolate (New York, NY) Nouvelle
American: www.keeschocolates.com

Knipschildt Chocolatier (South Norwalk, CT)
Belgian: www.knipschildt.com

L.A. Burdick (Walpole, NH) Nouvelle American:
www.burdickchocolate.com

Ladurée (Paris, France) Belgian: www.laduree.com

La Maison du Chocolat (Paris, France) French:
www.lamaisonduchocolat.com

L'Artisan du Chocolat (Ashford Kent, England)
French: www.artisanduchocolat.com

Le Roux (Quiberon, France) French:
www.chocolatleroux.com

Lillie Belle Farms (Jacksonville, OR) Nouvelle
American: www.lilliebellefarms.com

MarieBelle (New York, NY) Belgian:
www.mariebelle.com

Mary Chocolatier (Belgium) Belgian:
www.marychocolatier.com

Mary's Chocolates (Japan) Asian-Influenced
French: www.mary.co.jp

Neuhaus (Belgium) Belgian: www.neuhaus.be

Norman Love Confections (Fort Myers, FL)
Nouvelle American: www.normanlove
confections.com

Patrick Roger (Sceaux, France) French:
www.patrickroger.com

Pralus (Roanne, France) French:
www.chocolats-pralus.com

Pierre Hermé (Paris, France) French:
www.pierreherme.com

Recchiuti Confections (San Francisco, CA)
Nouvelle American: www.recchiuti.com

Richart Design et Chocolat (Paris, France)
French: www.richart-chocolates.com

Rococo (London, England) French:
www.rococochocolates.com

Teuscher (Zurich, Switzerland) Belgian:
www.teuscher.com

Vosges Haut Chocolat (Chicago, IL) French:
www.vosgeschocolate.com

Woodhouse Chocolate (Saint Helena, CA)
Belgian: www.woodhousechocolate.com

GOURMET

Butlers Chocolates (Dublin, Ireland) Belgian:
www.butlerschocolates.com

Garrison Confections (Providence, RI) Nouvelle
American: www.garrisonconfections.com

Godiva Chocolatier (Gold—New York, NY)
Belgian: www.godiva.com

Joseph Schmidt Confections (San Francisco, CA)
Belgian: www.josephschmidtconfections.com

Lake Champlain Chocolate Company (Burlington, VT)
Belgian: www.lakechamplainchocolates.com

Leonidas (S.A. Confiserie Leonidas) (Brussels,
Belgium) Belgian: www.leonidas-chocolate.com

Martine's Chocolates (New York, NY) Belgian:
www.martineschocolates.com

Mazet de Montargis (Montargis, France)
French: www.mazetconfiseur.com

Michel Cluizel (Damville, France) French:
www.chocolatmichelcluizel.com

Neuhaus (Belgium) Belgian: www.neuhaus.be

Tumbador Chocolate (Brooklyn, NY) French:
www.tumbadorchocolate.com

Venchi (Castelletto Stura, Italy) Belgian:
www.venchi.it

MASS-MARKET PREMIUM

Fannie May/Fannie Farmer (Chicago, IL)
American: www. fanniemay.com

See's Candies (Carson, CA) American:
www.sees.com

As a general rule, I don't advise buying boxes of chocolates in any location other than a chocolate shop, and only those where you can ask when the box was packed. If it's been a while (more than a week) and you know the chocolates won't be eaten right away, ask the server to make a box up for you on the spot. It will probably cost more than the preselected box, but the increase in quality will more than offset the increase in price.

If you find yourself in a position where you have no alternative but to buy a preselected box of chocolates, at least take a few moments to look at the ingredients list. (Refer to page 115 for details about what to look for in good chocolates—and what to avoid.)

It's a Truffle, but Is It *Chocolate*?

Following is the ingredient list from a very popular box of "chocolates" being sold at a recent chocolate event. Based on the ingredients (listed in order below), the reason for its popularity could not have been the product's quality; it had to be the price: two boxes of twenty-two truffles cost $10.

Nowhere on the box was the word *chocolate* used to describe the truffles.

Why not? Because in order to use the word chocolate (instead of, for example, chocolate-flavored) a product has to contain a minimum amount of cocoa. In these truffles, the relatively small amount of cocoa contained in the low-fat cocoa does not meet the minimum requirements, so the word chocolate can't be used to describe them.

INGREDIENTS
partially hydrogenated vegetable oils, sugar, low-fat cocoa, whey powder, cocoa powder, emulsifier (soy lecithin), natural flavor (vanilla)

HOW TO BUY CHOCOLATES FOR GIVING

When you are buying chocolates for others, the single most important thing is to make sure you show that you've been paying attention to the likes and dislikes of the recipient. When buying chocolate as a gift, consider the following:

• If you know that the recipient is *not* an adventurous eater (sushi is never mentioned when the two of you are trying to decide where to go for dinner), it's probably best to stay away from exotic flavors and stick to old favorites like plain ganaches and caramels.

• If you know that the recipient *is* an adventurous eater (not only does she like sushi but she's into uni, tako, and ika), by all means go for exotic flavors.

• If you have *no idea* what the recipient's likes and dislikes are, buy a selection of pieces that you like and tell a story about why you chose them. "I ate chocolates like these on vacation in Rome and wanted to share them with you."

• Try not to gift chocolate that you would not buy for yourself. I know it's hard to let go of a box of truffles you really love, but meaningful gifts often involve small sacrifices. Besides, the recipient might share with you.

• Always choose quality over quantity. Two pieces of exquisite chocolate that are packaged beautifully and that come with a story about why you chose those particular two pieces are worth a lot more than a two-pound box you can pick up at the local supermarket on the way home from the office. •

4.

Sophisticated Pairings

CHOCOLATE WITH WINE AND OTHER DELIGHTFUL COMBINATIONS

IT ALL COMES DOWN TO THIS. ✳ You've tasted dozens and dozens of chocolates, taking copious tasting notes along the way and learning where each chocolate came from and how it was made, you have a good idea of what you like in a chocolate (and why), and you've sought out and discovered the best chocolatiers in your area. It's definitely time to enjoy your favorite bars and confections in a way that shows them off to their best advantage—highlighting their brightest attributes and making every food and drink that comes before or after them seem better by association.

Wine plus chocolate seems like a match made in heaven, but finding good pairings is more challenging—and more fun—than it might seem at first blush. The traditional advice—red wines and ports go with dark chocolate—is just about as helpful as the old saw that red wine goes with meat and white wine goes with fish, and just as exciting. While that's a fine place to start if you have no other ideas (read on and you'll be introduced to loads of them), the common wisdom is just too vague to be useful to a true chocophile—and often it's simply wrong.

PAIRING WINES AND CHOCOLATES

❋

Grapes

Cocoa beans

Both chocolates and wines are varietal foods, which means that where the beans or grapes are grown and what type of beans or grapes are used affects the taste of the chocolate or the wine made with them. Furthermore, the taste can change from harvest to harvest and year to year. Pairings are further complicated because chocolates (even those with the same cocoa content) have very different levels of sweetness, which affects the way the chocolates work with or against certain wines. Some chocolate companies have published guidelines that suggest that any 55 percent dark chocolate will go with any Cabernet Sauvignon, and that any 56 percent dark chocolate will go with any Pinot Noir. But whose 55 percent dark chocolate? And which Cab from what growing region and from what vintage? And what about *white* wines?

Your exploration of chocolate and wine pairings will be most fun if you make decidedly *un*conventional choices. I can guarantee you'll come across some clunker pairings, but you are also likely to come across some great, unexpected ones.

TWO DIFFERENT APPROACHES TO PAIRING CHOCOLATE WITH WINE

Traditionally, food and wine pairing is based either on matching up *complementary* flavors or *contrasting* flavors.

The traditional pairing of red wines and dark chocolates is an example of using the complementary approach. I've found, however, that it doesn't work very often, because the tannins in red wine more often than not fight the tannins in dark chocolate, resulting in an unpleasant battle of flavors in the mouth. This can be especially true for big, bold wines that can be drunk quite young and higher-cocoa-content dark chocolates.

In my wine and chocolate pairing classes, I pair red wines and milk chocolates (an example of using the contrasting approach) and white wines with dark chocolates. In my experience, the milk fat in milk chocolate reduces the effect of the bitter and astringent tannins in the red wines, taming them and making the pairings harmonious instead of clashing. With white wines and dark chocolates, it's best to stay away from acidic wines such as Sauvignon Blancs and Fumé Blancs or blends that contain large percentages of these grapes. Chardonnays can work well if you stay away from extremes; those aged in stainless steel often lack a certain breadth and roundness of flavor, which makes them fall flat with most chocolates, whereas very oak-y Chardonnays (common in Chardonnays from California) tend to overpower chocolate. Semi-dry (or half-sweet) wines made with Gewürztraminer, Riesling, and Scheurebe (a cross between Riesling and Sylvaner) grapes are good choices and often possess a slight effervescence that is very appealing; their floral aromas are often perfect complements to blended semisweet dark chocolates.

When it comes to sparkling wines, I prefer Proseccos to Champagnes. As a group, Proseccos have a tendency to be less acidic than Champagnes and therefore have a better chance of pairing well with chocolate.

COMPLEMENTS =
red wine +
dark chocolate

white wine +
milk chocolate

CONTRASTS =
red wine +
milk chocolate

white wine +
dark chocolate

HOW TO TASTE WINE AND CHOCOLATE TOGETHER

Two problems: (1) Small amounts of water and chocolate don't mix (the chocolate seizes and the texture becomes chunky), and cold liquids also affect the texture of chocolate negatively; (2) wines should be served at their ideal temperature, which, especially for whites, is too cold to make pairing them with chocolate easy. In order to taste chocolate and wine together enjoyably, these obstacles must be overcome.

To do this, place a piece of chocolate in your mouth and chew it until it has melted completely, working the chocolate with your tongue to incorporate saliva from your mouth. The idea is to mix in enough warm liquid so that adding cold liquid—the wine—won't be such a shock to the chocolate and cause it to seize. When the chocolate has a thin consistency, take a sip of wine—about the same amount of wine as the amount of chocolate in your mouth.

Mix the wine and the chocolate together in your mouth by gently swishing, paying attention to the taste and texture sensations in your mouth before swallowing the wine and the chocolate. Wait at least ten seconds after swallowing the chocolate and wine before taking a small sip of wine to rinse any leftover chocolate from your mouth.

DISCOVERING YOUR OWN GREAT WINE AND CHOCOLATE PAIRINGS

The only way to develop confidence in your sense of taste is practice. In Chapter 1, I introduced the pyramid as a way to organize your tasting to quickly arrive at a clear understanding of what you like. When pairing wines and chocolates, I use a similar approach.

Start off with either wines you know and like or chocolates you know and like. Especially when you are new to chocolate and wine pairing, making sure that one half of the pairing is a known entity will make it easier to figure out what about a pairing is or isn't working.

Mix the wine and chocolate by gently swishing them in your mouth.

First taste the wines and chocolates individually and separately. Before you begin pairing, introduce your mouth to what you will be pairing. You can taste the wines and chocolates in any order you want, but it's wise to stick with small amounts and cleanse your palate between tastes. Concentrate on identifying the most obvious sense impressions. Is the wine acidic, tannic, fruity, spicy? Does it start out acidic and end soft, or vice versa? Don't worry too much about identifying the specific fruit or spice flavors at this point. Do the same thing for the chocolate: Is it sweet, acidic, tannic or astrigent, fruity, caramelly? Does it have a long finish?

Use a many-to-one organizational approach, not a one-to-one approach. Rather than trying to guess in advance what pairings might work, pair multiple wines against a single chocolate, or multiple chocolates against a single wine. In my pairing classes, I usually pair one red wine and three milk chocolates, and then three white wines and one dark chocolate. If I am teaching an advanced class, I might also pair three red wines and one dark chocolate, and then one white wine and three milk chocolates. When I pair multiple wines with a single chocolate, I almost always use very different wines rather than three wines of the same general type.

A typical white wine selection would include a sparkling wine such as a Prosecco, a dry white wine from the Riesling or Gewürztraminer family, and a sweet wine that is not a late-harvest dessert wine, such as a Jurançon. I like to mix and match wines from all over the world. As for red wines, I like pairing 100 percent Grenaches with milk chocolates, but find that blended reds with less than 50 percent of any single grape variety work better with dark chocolates than do 100 percent varietals.

Start out with the general and move to the more specific. When you are categorizing your sense impressions, first ask yourself:

• Do I like the pairing?

The next questions to consider are:

• Does the wine make the chocolate taste better or worse?
• Does the chocolate make the wine taste better or worse?

Once you've arrived at the answers to those three questions, you can start trying to identify what it is about the pairing that either works or doesn't work. It is useful to try to identify what you don't like about a pairing, because those sense impressions are the ones that will help you steer away from pairings that are not likely to delight.

Some of the most common reasons for not liking a pairing are:

• The wine overpowered the chocolate.
• The chocolate overpowered the wine.
• The chocolate made the wine taste bitter (or sour).
• The acidity in the wine made the chocolate aftertaste unpleasant.

Other Wines to Consider

Late-harvest dessert wines of every stripe pair well with most dark and milk chocolates, as well as many truffles. When pairing, however, make sure that any flavor in the chocolate or truffle complements the flavors in the wine.

Ports are fortified wines (wines that have had alcohol added to them). Port is the oldest controlled appellation in the world, and legally only wines in this style that are made in Portugal can properly be called Port. When pairing Ports with chocolate,

I err on the side of age, preferring to pair with older Ports that have mellowed and have developed more complex flavors. I enjoy tasting Ports with truffles whose centers complement the flavors in the Ports.

There is a class of wines made from a grape called Monastrell (aka Mourvedre) that is called *dulce*, or sweet, *Monastrell*. I have found that many of these pair well with chocolate, especially warm chocolate desserts that also include caramel.

+

Port

PAIRING DISTILLED SPIRITS AND CHOCOLATES

✳

I have had mixed results pairing distilled spirits with chocolate. In general, I have found that clear spirits such as gin, vodka, tequila, white rum, and especially fruit brandies are much harder to pair harmoniously with chocolate than brown spirits such as Scotches, Bourbons, dark rums, Cognacs, and Armagnacs.

Distilled fruit brandies such as poire and kirschwasser (cherry brandy), can work very well as flavorings in ganache, but as drinks they are usually just too harsh and alcoholic to be taken with chocolate, as they completely dominate the chocolate in an unpleasant way. However, there are some exceptions. Several years ago I was given a small bottle of aged wild kirschwasser that had mellowed enough to make it work with dark, fruity ganaches.

Gins are flavored with juniper berries, which gives them a distinct taste but makes pairing difficult. There used to be a chocolate from the Dominican Republic with a distinct green-olive note, so maybe a pairing with gin would have created an unusual chocolate Martini (but probably not).

Plain vodkas are too neutral to pair with chocolate, as the chocolate flavor overwhelms whatever flavor the vodka does possess. Flavored vodkas can often be paired with chocolates of like or complementary flavors; if you like spicy chocolates, a chili-infused vodka can provide a similar bite when taken alongside a plain chocolate or plain ganache.

Clear rums, although they often do have some flavor, are usually best used as mixers. Dark rums, especially aged rums that are good "sipping" rums, often pair well with plain dark chocolate as well as milk chocolate with heavy caramel notes and truffles filled with praliné.

Chocolate

+

Scotch

✳

Bourbon

✳

Dark rum

✳

Cognac

✳

Armagnac

Brown spirits, because of their complex flavors and sweetness (compared with clear spirits), often pair will with chocolates. Even distinctive single-malt Scotches can pair well, especially with chocolates in the 80-percent-plus cocoa-content range. You'll be successful sooner if you start your brown spirit pairing adventures with choices you can drink "neat"—without mixers or ice.

THE CHOCOLATE MARTINI

Modern Martinis come in all flavors and levels of sweetness, but the true Martini—whether made with vodka or gin—is very dry. At its extreme, the open bottle of vermouth is simply waved over the top of the glass, perhaps imparting some elusive aroma but not even a hint of sweetness.

The base alcohol of most chocolate "Martinis" (many would consider it heresy to use the word to refer to anything other than gin and vermouth) is sweet—either a creme (a sweetened, flavored neutral spirit) or a cream (flavored spirits blended with dairy cream) liqueur. Because the base alcohol is sweet, many chocolate Martinis start out at a level of sweetness far beyond anything most Martini connoisseurs would consider to be drinkable. And then chocolate is added which pushes it still further over the edge.

There are several ways to make chocolate Martinis that are not sweet. Choose the method that suits your palate and your patience, but consider experimenting with the other methods as well—you might be pleasantly surprised.

The first is to start out with a chocolate-flavored vodka (such as Van Gogh) that has not been sweetened. There are several other brands available, but they do not tend to show up in less-well-stocked liquor stores. If you can't find unsweetened chocolate-flavored vodka, you can ask for a special order.

An artfully mixed chocolate Martini—shaken or stirred— is a thing of beauty.

The other way is to make your own base by infusing a high-quality plain vodka with cocoa nibs. This works best using freshly roasted nibs, and I can't stress enough the importance of using a high-quality vodka: even the best cocoa nibs will not make a substandard vodka taste good. The ratio of nibs to vodka and the length of time to infuse is a matter of personal preference. Replace 100 milliliters (about four ounces) of a 750-milliliter bottle of vodka with a roughly equal amount of nibs, cap the bottle, and let the vodka infuse for three days, shaking the bottle once daily. After three days, give it a taste. If you want more chocolate flavor, let the vodka infuse for a few more days. When the infused vodka attains a flavor you like, strain the vodka through several layers of cheesecloth to remove the nibs and any sediment. The result will be a beautiful mahogany-colored, unsweetened, chocolate-flavored vodka of the highest quality.

(It is also possible to infuse some rums and tequilas using this technique. As with vodka, it's best to start out with a very-high-quality liquor. I have had the best experiences with "silver" rums as well as silver and gold tequilas. If you can easily drink the spirit neat, and it has no harsh alcoholic bite, you can use it in a cocoa infusion.)

To make a chocolate Martini, simply fill a cocktail shaker with ice, add the chocolate-flavored vodka, stir, and strain into a cocktail glass garnished with chocolate shavings, chocolate syrup, or (my favorite) cocoa powder. Other garnishes include coffee beans and lemon or orange peel twists. The chocolate Martini can also be flavored using liqueurs. Orange liqueurs work very well, as do anise-flavored ones, but be sure to use them very sparingly so that their sweetness does not overpower the wonderful cocoa flavor.

CHOCOPHILE FACT
Chocolate is used to (imperfectly) mask the flavor of decoctions made with bitter herbs used in Ecuadorian shamanistic rituals.

✳

PAIRING LIQUEURS AND CHOCOLATES

✳

Liqueurs (which are sweeter than plain distilled spirits) and chocolate can be great together, especially when you choose liqueurs whose flavors are already known to work well with chocolate:

- Fruits: orange, raspberry
- Spices: anise
- Nuts: almond, walnut

- Herbs: mint
- Coffee

Cream liqueurs also pair well with chocolate. You don't need to add anything to them to enjoy them with chocolate; just pair complementary flavors. Unless your palate runs to the very sweet, you'll have better luck pairing cream liqueurs with dark chocolates than with milk chocolates. There are quite a few liqueurs flavored with bitter herbs, but as I find most of them so difficult to drink I can't imagine wasting good chocolate trying to come up with a good match.

Prosecco and Goat Cheese Truffles

One of my favorite unusual truffles is made with a ganache of white chocolate, goat cheese, Champagne, and black pepper. The ganache balls are dipped in dark chocolate and then dusted with roasted herbs. You either really like these or you don't like them at all, but you'll never know for sure until you try them.

I was first introduced to these at an outdoor reception for Christopher Norman Chocolates, the chocolatier who made them, and they were paired with Prosecco, which is lighter and tends to be less acidic than Champagne. If you want to try pairing a white wine with these, look for something that is medium- to full-bodied. A wine with herbal and fruity notes (especially pear) should work well—try a *halbtrocken* ("half-dry") Scheurebe from Germany.

MORE GREAT PAIRINGS

✳

The purpose of this section is to get you thinking imaginatively when it comes to pairings. I once attended a class with Albert Adria, the celebrated pastry chef, who said that he has taste memory for over eight hundred herbs, spices, and other ingredients. Often, he says, he can "visualize" what a dish will taste like by imaging the combinations of flavors in his mouth. While few of us have this capability, we all do have some taste memory and we can use it to imagine new combinations.

STRAWBERRIES AND CHOCOLATE

Several years ago, I was looking for a new way to serve chocolate with strawberries for an event. I could easily do chocolate-covered strawberries, but I was looking for a very different form of presentation and one in which I could easily introduce at least one other, unexpected flavor.

Of course, everyone knows that chocolate and strawberries go together. I had also seen recipes in which strawberries were seasoned with freshly ground black pepper and others in which balsamic vinegar was drizzled over strawberries. Because I know what all the individual ingredients taste like, I could imagine how they might all go together. It turns out that they go together very well.

Using a mandoline, or a very sharp knife, julienne (cut into matchsticks) very ripe strawberries. Put them in a glass bowl with balsamic vinegar and sugar to taste. Toss gently just until the sugar crystals are dissolved. Spoon the strawberries into prepared bite-sized chocolate cups (they need to be small enough so that you can put the whole thing in your mouth in one bite), and then sprinkle each with a little fresh ground black pepper. This just might be my favorite way to enjoy chocolate with strawberries.

Chocolate cups can now often be found in better gourmet stores, often labeled as chocolate-liqueur cups. If you can't find them locally, you can make them yourself using melted, untempered chocolate, as long as you're going to use them within a couple of hours. To make them you'll need to find a small mold with a flat bottom—plastic ice-cube trays work well, especially if you find one that makes small cubes. Pour cooled melted chocolate into a room-temperature mold and wait for the chocolate to firm up slightly. Pour out the excess chocolate and scrape (using a spatula) excess chocolate off the top of the mold. Place the tray in the fridge for a few minutes, and the chocolate cups should just pop out. (It pays to be patient.) Whatever you do, don't clean these molds with detergent. The thin film of cocoa butter left in the mold after rinsing will help future cups pop out of the mold with ease and contribute a nice shine.

POMEGRANATE KIR AND POMEGRANATE GANACHE TRUFFLE

A pomegranate kir is made by pouring pomegranate liqueur into a Champagne glass and filling the glass with a sparkling wine such as Prosecco (my favorite) or Champagne. This drink goes nicely with a pomegranate ganache truffle.

If you want to pair a kir with another type of truffle, simply match the liqueur you are using to flavor the kir with the flavor of the ganache in the truffle.

CHOCOLATE IN CONDIMENTS

Dark chocolate and balsamic vinegar go surprisingly well together, especially when spices, herbs, garlic, or other flavorings are added. Start off with a 4:1 mix of balsamic vinegar to grated chocolate, warming the vinegar to melt the chocolate, and sweetening to taste. For spices, start with one-half teaspoon per cup (240 ml) of vinegar, adjusting to suit your personal taste and the strength of the spices used. The cocoa butter in the chocolate

> **Compromises are for relationships, not chocolate.**
>
> —with apologies to Sir Robert Caywood

Try adding some chocolate or cocoa powder to your chili or stew.

Pairing Beers and Chocolates

The easiest way to pair beer with chocolate (in my opinion) is to pair beer with foods that have chocolate as an ingredient. One of my tricks for making really great chili is to add cocoa powder at the last minute; this chocolate chili goes very well with many different styles of beers.

There are some beers that seem to be made to pair with chocolate— stouts and porters, in particular, because of their complex flavor profiles, which often include chocolate and caramel notes, as well as their relative lack of carbonation. I have more success pairing stouts and porters with milk chocolates than with darks. Belgian-style Lambics, even the fruit-flavored ones, often pair well with dark chocolates.

will add quite a bit of body to the sauce, so it may need to be warmed before serving. The sauce can be used as a glaze for meat or vegetables, as an edible decoration on a plate, or as a condiment. It can even be used on cut fruit, depending on the spice used—cinnamon and strawberries, for example, is a great combination. Chocolate can also be used to make sophisticated versions of ketchup, mayonnaise, and mustard. (I have not tried it in pickle relish and I am not likely to unless I am *really* bored one day.)

CHOCOLATE IN CHILI OR STEW

One of the secrets to a great New Orleans–style gumbo is filé, or ground sassafras root. The sassafras acts as a thickener but it also lends a vegetal earthiness to the gumbo that provides a solid foundation for all of the other flavors. A little bit of chocolate (or cocoa powder) added to chili or stew just before serving can similarly fill out the bottom of the dish and make it more substantial without tasting at all like chocolate.

One of my favorite dry spice rubs contains my seven Cs—fine-ground espresso coffee beans, ground cocoa nibs (grind them together with the salt and sugar so they don't turn into a paste), ground coriander, ground cumin, ground celery seed, ground dried chipotles, and cheese (grated Parmesan)—plus dried thyme, sugar, salt, and black pepper. This is great on many types of fish and shrimp as well as pork.

TASTING AND PAIRING WITH CONFIDENCE

✳

Just as I was wrapping up work on the manuscript for *Discover Chocolate*, I was asked to organize a wine and chocolate pairing event for the New York Chapter of les Dames d'Escoffier, a culinary leadership organization composed of women who have achieved success in their profession and who also contribute to their communities. The tasting was hosted by Harriet Lembeck, a very highly respected wine educator. Although I have been doing these wine and chocolate pairing classes for several years, this was the first time I was going to be testing my approach and knowledge on such an educated audience; I was more than a little apprehensive.

Things got off to a rough start when two of the three bottles of one of the wines I selected had oxidized and were not drinkable. At first, only a few of les Dames bought into my thesis that red wines are easier to pair with milk chocolates, but by the end of the evening everyone was convinced that, by following the conventional wisdom (red wines and ports go with dark chocolates), they were limiting themselves for no good reason. It is my sincere hope that you will use the information in this chapter (and in the rest of *Discover Chocolate*) to explore new territories of taste, personal enjoyment, and expression. •

FLAVOR COMBINATIONS TO SAVOR

STRAWBERRIES AND CHOCOLATE

Using a mandoline or a very sharp knife, cut very ripe strawberries into match-sticks. Put them in a glass bowl with balsamic vinegar and sugar to taste. Toss gently just until the sugar crystals dissolve. Spoon the strawberries into prepared bite-sized chocolate cups, and then sprinkle each with a little fresh ground black pepper.

DARK CHOCOLATE WITH BALSAMIC

Start off with a 4:1 mix of balsamic vinegar to grated chocolate, warming the vinegar to melt the chocolate, and sweetening to taste. For spices, start with one-half teaspoon per cup (240 ml) of vinegar, adjusting to suit your personal taste and the strength of the spices used.

CHOCOLATE CUPS

Find a small mold with a flat bottom— plastic ice-cube trays work well, especially if you hunt one up that makes small cubes. Pour cooled melted chocolate into a room-temperature mold and wait ten to fifteen seconds for the chocolate to firm up. Pour out the excess chocolate and scrape (using a spatula) excess chocolate off the top of the mold. Pop the tray into the fridge for a few minutes, and the chocolate cups should just pop out.

CHOCOLATE CHILI

A little bit of chocolate (or cocoa powder) added to chili or stew just before serving can similarly fill out the bottom of the dish and make it more substantial without tasting at all like chocolate.

CHOCOLATE SPICE RUB

In a grinder, fine-ground espresso coffee beans and cocoa nibs (grind them together with the salt and sugar so they don't turn into a paste), coriander, cumin, celery seed, dried chipotles, and cheese (grated Parmesan)—plus dried thyme, sugar, salt, and black pepper. This is great on many types of fish and shrimp as well as pork.

POMEGRANATE KIR

Pour pomegranate liqueur into a Champagne glass and fill with a sparkling wine.

Appendix

MAPS OF THE MOST IMPORTANT COCOA-PRODUCING COUNTRIES

✳

THE COCOA BELT　　▓ Cocoa-Producing Countries　　····· The Tropical Belt

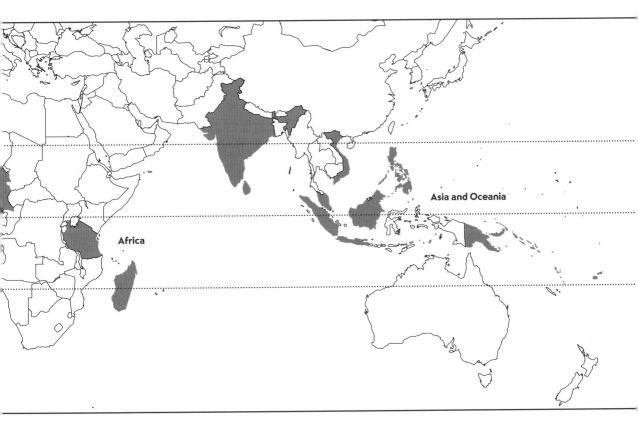

Africa

Asia and Oceania

REGION
Asia and Oceania

COCOA-PRODUCING COUNTRIES IN REGION
Fiji, India, Indonesia (Java, Sumatra), Borneo (Kalimantan), Malaysia, Papua New Guinea, Philippines, Samoa, Solomon Islands, Sri Lanka (Ceylon), Vanuatu, Vietnam

TYPES OF BEANS GROWN
Forastero, Trinitario

PERCENTAGE OF WORLD CROP
< 10%

ASIA AND OCEANIA ▢ Major Producers ▢ Minor Producers

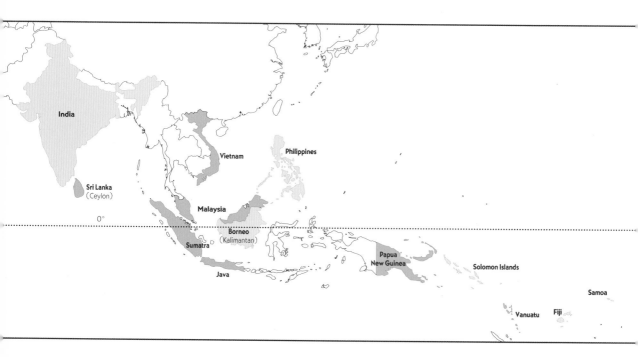

REGION
The Americas

COCOA-PRODUCING COUNTRIES IN REGION
Belize, Bolivia, Brazil, Colombia, Costa Rica, Cuba, Dominica, Dominican Republic, Ecuador, El Salvador, Grenada, Guatemala, Haiti, Honduras, Jamaica, Mexico, Nicaragua, Panama, Peru, Puerto Rico, St. Lucia, St. Vincent/Grenadines, Suriname, Trinidad/Tobago, U.S. (Hawaii), Venezuela

TYPES OF BEANS GROWN
Criollo, Forastero, Trinitario

PERCENTAGE OF WORLD CROP
< 10%

THE AMERICAS □ Major Producers □ Minor Producers

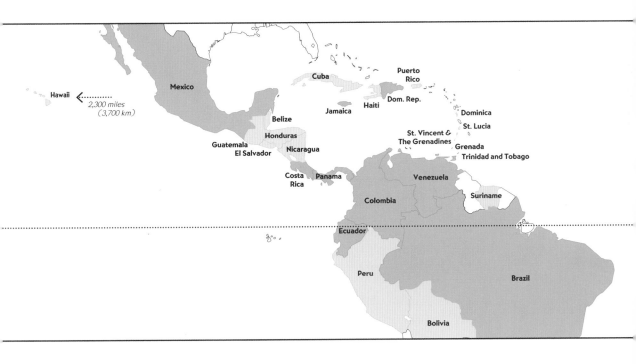

REGION
Africa

COCOA-PRODUCING COUNTRIES IN REGION
Cameroon, Ghana, Ivory Coast, Madagascar, Nigeria, Sao Tome/Principe,
Tanzania

TYPES OF BEANS GROWN
Forastero, Trinitario

PERCENTAGE OF WORLD CROP
> 80%

AFRICA   ▢ Major Producers   ▢ Minor Producers

Ivory Coast
Ghana
Nigeria
Cameroon
Sao Tome & Principe
0°
Tanzania
Madagascar

GLOSSARY: THE LANGUAGE OF CHOCOLATE

❋

"If you are not feeling well, if you have not
slept, chocolate will revive you. But you have
no chocolate! I think of that again and again!
My dear, how will you ever manage?"

—Marquise de Sevigne,
fifteenth-century French writer and lady of fashion

Words in bold are defined within the glossary.

ANTIOXIDANTS: Chemicals that reduce the rate of oxidative stress on cells in the body. Antioxidants are widely used as ingredients in dietary supplements taken for health purposes such as preventing cancer and heart disease. Cacao has one of the highest concentrations of antioxidants of all plants.

ARRIBA: Arriba is the name given to the unique flavor of the Nacional cocoa bean. Arriba is often used as a synonym for Nacional, but this is not correct usage.

BAKING CHOCOLATE: **Chocolate** with no sugar added. Also called unsweetened chocolate. Some unsweetened/baking chocolates contain dairy ingredients (butter oil, milk fat) and the only way to tell is to check the label. Dairy ingredients are added to stabilize the **cocoa butter** crystals to keep them from **blooming**.

BITTERSWEET CHOCOLATE: There is no agreement on what constitutes a bittersweet **chocolate**; it is not based either on sugar or **cocoa content**—there is no dividing line between **semisweet chocolate** and bittersweet chocolate. Bitterness in chocolate is a result of the way cocoa beans are roasted. The more heavily roasted a cocoa bean is, the more burnt/bitter flavors develop. It is possible to have a very-high-**cocoa**-**content** chocolate that is not bitter because the beans have not been burnt during roasting.

BLEND, BLENDING: The process of mixing different types of beans, each roasted a specific way, to create a specific **chocolate** flavor, also called a flavor profile. Blending happens for two other reasons: to control costs and to create new flavor profiles that don't occur naturally. Sometimes roasted beans are blended before grinding. Sometimes cocoa liquors are blended before refining, and sometimes **chocolatiers** blend finished **couvertures** because their volume requirements are too small to justify the cost of developing and manufacturing a custom blend.

BLOOM: A surface condition of **chocolate** that is the result of improper storage or handling. A chocolate that exhibits signs of either **cocoa butter bloom** or **sugar bloom** is said to have bloomed.

CACAO: From the Mayan hieroglyph pronounced "ka KA wa." *Cacao* is the familiar name given to the tree, fruit, and seeds of *Theobroma cacao* (or *T. cacao*), a tropical plant that grows up to 49 feet (15 meters) tall that is the source of the primary raw material used to make **chocolate**. Today, the word *cocoa* is often used to refer to cacao, and this can be attributed to a transcription error when a sixteenth-century manuscript was being copied and translated.

CARAMEL: At its simplest, caramel is cooked sugar, although many recipes for caramel call for additional ingredients. Depending on the ingredients and the temperature to which it is cooked, caramel can attain many different textures, making it a very versatile ingredient to work with. The traditional **praliné** is a nut cooked in boiling (caramelizing) sugar.

CHOCOLATE: A mixture of **cocoa liquor** (ground cocoa beans) and, optionally, **cocoa butter**, sugar, lecithin, and/or vanilla. The term is also used to refer to **truffles**, bon bons, and pralines.

CHOCOLATE LIQUOR: **Cocoa liquor**.

CHOCOLATE MANUFACTURER: A person or company that makes chocolate starting from raw cocoa beans. Very few chocolate manufacturers are also **chocolatiers**.

CHOCOLATIER: A person or company that makes **truffles** (also called bon bons and pralines) using **chocolate** and other ingredients. Very few chocolatiers are also **chocolate manufacturers**. Most chocolatiers purchase chocolate in bulk and melt it down before using it.

COCOA BUTTER: A yellow-white fat derived from cocoa beans. By weight, the cocoa bean is approximately 50 percent fat, though it can range between 45 and 55 percent. The percentage of cocoa butter (and other fats and emulsifiers) in a **chocolate** contributes to the feeling of creaminess in the mouth. **Couverture** chocolates contain a higher percentage of cocoa butter so they are thinner when they melt. Although technically cocoa butter is a saturated fat, because of its unique chemical makeup it does not contribute to elevated levels of blood cholesterol.

COCOA BUTTER BLOOM: A thin, translucent white coating over a bar of **chocolate** or a chocolate confection. Cocoa butter bloom is the result of improper storage, often when a piece becomes too warm and then is cooled, suddenly causing some of the **cocoa butter** to escape from the chocolate and crystallize on the surface. Cocoa butter bloom certainly affects the visual appeal of a piece of chocolate and, depending on how bad it is and how long ago it happened, can also negatively affect taste and texture. Solid chocolate that has been bloomed can usually be melted and re-**tempered**, "fixing" it.

COCOA CONTENT: The total cocoa content of a **chocolate**, measured by percentage. The total content of a chocolate includes both the cocoa solids (powder) and the **cocoa butter** (fat). A typical chocolate bar with a 70 percent cocoa content is 70 percent cocoa (the exact ratio of solids to butter is usually not divulged), 28 to 29 percent sugar, and 1 to 2 percent lecithin and vanilla. Contrary to widespread belief, there is absolutely no relationship between cocoa content and chocolate quality.

COCOA LIQUOR: The thick (nonalcoholic) paste that is the result of the first grinding of cocoa beans. Cocoa liquor contains no added ingredients. Also called cocoa mass and chocolate liquor.

COCOA MASS: **Cocoa liquor**.

COCOA NIB: The "meat" of the cocoa bean that is left after the shell has been removed. The nib is what is ground to make chocolate. Cocoa nibs can also be eaten alone, raw or roasted.

CONCHE: Invented by Rudolph Lindt in 1879, the conche ushered in the modern era of **chocolate** making, enabling **chocolate manufacturers** for the first time to create a smooth, creamy product free of grit and harsh acidity. The conche gets its name from the shape of the original machine developed by Lindt. Today there are two main types of conches, longitudinal (like a bathtub) and vertical (like a front-loading washing machine). Conching improves the quality of chocolate by ensuring that there are no clumps of cocoa particles and that all particles are covered with **cocoa butter**, evaporating out any remaining water in the chocolate, and evaporating out any harsh flavors. In general, longer conching times are preferable to shorter conching times, but there is no magic minimum time: the composition of the chocolate and the intent of the chocolate maker ultimately determine the best optimum time needed to balance all of the sensory elements of the finished chocolate.

CREMINO: A type of **chocolate** confection characterized by three layers of dense **ganache**. The most common type of cremino has two **dark chocolate** layers sandwiching a **milk chocolate** layer. Often, especially in Italy, one or more of the layers is **gianduja**, a type of chocolate ganache made with hazelnut cream.

COUVERTURE: *Couverture* comes from the French word for "cover." Couverture **chocolates** are chocolates that are used, in part, to cover chocolate confections such as truffles. In order to be used this way, couverture chocolates need to be thinner than eating chocolate when it is melted, which means that couverture

chocolate contains a higher percentage of **cocoa butter** than chocolate that is made solely for eating. Because couvertures contain more cocoa butter, they have a creamier, more luscious mouth feel; many chocophiles prefer to eat couvertures.

CRIOLLO: The Criollo bean falls into the fine flavor category of cocoa bean. Criollo beans produce **chocolate** with more delicate and nuanced flavors than chocolate made with other types of beans. Criollo **cacao** trees are less resistant to disease, mature later, produce for fewer years, and produce fewer pods than **Forastero** trees. Perhaps the most highly prized Criollo variety is the Porcelana bean—it is certainly one of the rarest. There is some controversy over which came first, the Criollo or the Forastero. Recent DNA and archaeological research strongly indicate that Forastero is the original species and Criollo evolved from it, probably as a result of domestication and deliberate breeding.

DARK CHOCOLATE: Conventionally, dark chocolate is any chocolate that does not contain milk. However, there is no legal definition for dark chocolate and there are many "dark" chocolates that contain dairy ingredients, including butter oil and/or milk fat.

DRY, DRYING: Once **cacao** seeds have been fermented, they need to be dried to a moisture level of about 7 percent to preserve them for storage and shipping. Drier beans are too easily cracked in handling, and wetter beans are susceptible to molds and mildew. Ideally, drying happens in the sun over the course of three to seven days. However, some climates make this difficult, and there are a variety of forced drying methods available. Some, most notably the forced drying of beans using heat generated from fires, has the potential to contaminate the beans with smoky flavors. The method of drying has other impacts on flavor development, particularly with respect to the amount of residual acetic acid (vinegar) left in the beans.

ENROBED TRUFFLE: See A Field Guide to Truffles, page 42.

FERMENT, FERMENTATION: Once **cacao** pods have been harvested and the seeds removed, the beans need to be fermented before being dried. Fermentation is one of the most important aspects of **chocolate** flavor development. Unfermented beans do not develop chocolate flavor at all. Underfermented beans can be harsh, acidic, and astringent; overfermented beans generate rotten off flavors reminiscent of smoked ham that has been pickled. Fermentation takes place over three to seven days depending on the type of beans being fermented, the quantity of beans being fermented, the method used, and environmental conditions including the differential between day-time high and nighttime low temperatures.

FORASTERO: The Forastero bean falls into the ordinary, or bulk, category of **cacao** bean. Forastero beans produce **chocolate** that is more robust in flavor than that produced by Criollo beans. Forastero trees are hardier, mature earlier, produce for more years, and produce more pods than Criollo trees. Forastero beans now account for more than 95 percent of the world crop.

GANACHE: A classic ganache is a mixture of cream and **chocolate**. Ganaches can be made with other fats. Some ganaches substitute oils such as olive oil for the cream to impart an unusual flavor and to improve shelf life. Butter, especially high-fat butter, is used to improve mouth feel and add richness, though at the expense of shelf life. Other ingredients that can be added to ganaches include flavorings, sweeteners, and preservatives.

GIANDUJA: Italian in origin, gianduja is a mixture of hazelnut cream (roasted hazelnuts ground to a very thin paste) and **chocolate**, usually, but not necessarily, **milk chocolate**.

GUITAR: A device used to cut **ganache**, **caramel**, and **pralinés** into equal-sized pieces. Guitars have a base and a hinged frame that has thin wires strung across it (which is where it gets its name). The filling to be cut is placed on the base of the guitar and oriented properly, and then the frame with the wires is lowered, cutting the filling into strips. The strips are rotated 90 degrees and then cut again. Guitars have removable frames with cutting wires strung to create pieces in different sizes.

HAND-ROLLED TRUFFLE: See A Field Guide to Truffles, page 42.

MELANGEUR: French for "mixer." Melangeurs are used to grind cocoa beans into cocoa liquor. They consist of a circular tank within which large stone rollers rotate.

METATE: Pronounced "meh-TAH-tay." A metate is a curved stone on three short legs on which **cocoa beans** are traditionally ground. **Roasted**, **winnowed** beans are set on the surface of the metate, which is often placed over a small fire to warm the stone. A stone roller is used to crush the beans into a coarse, gritty paste, into which other ingredients (sugar, flavorings) are added. Because only a relatively light amount of pressure can be applied this way, it is impossible to grind the cocoa beans (and, if used, sugar crystals) to the point where they can't be felt on the tongue.

MILK CHOCOLATE: Milk Chocolate is a mixture of cocoa liquor, sugar, and milk and/or cream which has had much of the water removed from it. Most commonly, the milk used to make milk chocolate has either been dried or condensed. In the U.S., milk chocolate must contain (by weight) not less than 10 percent cocoa liquor, 3.39 percent milk fat, and 12 percent milk solids.

NACIONAL: The Nacional **cacao** bean is technically a **Forastero**, but it produces beans with strong **Criollo** characteristics and is actually a fine flavor variety. A properly processed, fermented, and dried Nacional bean grown in Ecuador has a very specific flavor redolent of jasmine and orange that has its own name—Arriba, so-called because these beans "arrived" from up-river of Guayaquil. (Nacional beans grown outside of Ecuador do not exhibit the full varietal strength of the bean due to differences in **terroir**.)

NAMED ORIGIN: A phrase used to describe a **chocolate** made with beans whose origin is specifically described. I coined the phrase in 2002 to replace **single origin** and pure origin. The term *single origin* can refer to a region as large as an entire country without identifying exactly where within the country the beans came from, which is misleading. For example, Venezuela has many different growing regions hundreds of miles apart, so "single-origin Venezuelan" is an incomplete description of where the beans come from. The origin of a named-origin chocolate can be very precise (for example, the Hacienda Helvesia in the Dominican Republic), a larger area or region (for example, the Sambirano valley in Madagascar or Lake Maracaibo in Venezuela), or a single country (for example, Indonesia, which consists of more than eighteen thousand islands, two of which—Sumatra and Java— are known for **cacao**).

NATURAL TRUFFLE: Also called *truffe nature*. See **Truffle**.

NIB: The meat of the **cocoa bean**. Nibs are the final result of the **roasting** and **winnowing** processes. Nibs are what are ground into **cocoa liquor** and made into **chocolate**.

PRALINE: Pronounced with a long *A* (as in *pray*), *praline* is the word the Belgians use for what the French call a **truffle** and Americans call a bon bon. Pronounced with a short *A* (as in *raw*), a praline resembles a cookie made from cooked sugar syrup with nuts in it. Not to be confused with **praliné**.

PRALINÉ: Pronounced "praw-lih-NAY." A mixture of nuts (typically almonds) cooked in boiled sugar and ground to a paste, which can either be very smooth or have a slight grainy texture, and mixed with **chocolate**. The development of praliné is attributed to the pastry chef to César, duc de Choiseul, comte du Plessis-Praslin (1602–1675).

REFINE: It is impossible to grind something the size of a **cocoa nib** to the point where it can't be felt on the tongue in one step—the size difference is too great. Chocolate manufacturing uses three steps to get cocoa particles to the necessary size: grinding, refining, and **conching**. Modern refiners are made up of three to five cooled steel rollers that the **cocoa liquor**—with any added ingredients, such as sugar, milk, and vanilla beans—is forced through. Each roller is smaller than the previous one, and the distance between rollers gets smaller and smaller, reducing particle size.

ROCHER: From the French word for "rock," a type of **chocolate** confection that looks like, well, a rock. The most famous rocher, from Ferrero, consists of a crunchy element (feuilletine, a crunchy, flaky pastry ingredient) surrounding a whole hazelnut that is covered in chocolate. Rochers are also made with slivered nuts (almonds are most commonly used) sometimes flavored with citrus zest, shaped into rough balls and covered in chocolate.

ROAST: Roasting is a key element in flavor development in **chocolate**. Once beans have been cleaned to remove foreign matter (stones, nails, sticks) and large clumps of beans, they are cooked (roasted). Cooking the beans causes sugars, proteins, and other chemicals in the bean to brown and caramelize, a process also known as the Maillard reaction. It is the caramelized flavors of the various chemicals in the bean that are the flavor of chocolate. Different types and sizes of beans are roasted separately—and differently—to develop the optimum flavor for each type of bean.

SEMISWEET CHOCOLATE: There is no agreement on what constitutes a semisweet **chocolate**; it is not based on cocoa or sugar content and there is no dividing line between semisweet chocolate and **bittersweet chocolate**: you can't say that chocolates with **cocoa contents** between (say) 39 percent and 69 percent are semisweet and anything over 70 percent is bittersweet.

SEVENTY PERCENT (70%): The **cocoa content** of a **chocolate**. Supposedly, chocolate with 70 percent cocoa content and above is "better" and/or "better for you" than chocolate with a cocoa content of 69 percent and below. There is no basis in fact for this belief. There is zero correlation between cocoa content and chocolate quality, and a 28-gram (1-ounce) serving of 70-percent-cocoa-content chocolate with no dairy ingredients contains nearly 10 grams of saturated fat (the recommended daily allowance for a 2,000-calorie diet is 20 grams of saturated fat per day).

SHELF LIFE: How long a product will keep before going bad. For **chocolate**, the shelf life is typically a year or more from the date of manufacture. Actual shelf life is dependent on whether the chocolate contains milk, the temperature and humidity at which the chocolate is stored, and other factors. For chocolate confections, the shelf life depends primarily on the amount of water in the center or filling (for example, in the cream and/or butter in the **ganache**), how much oxygen was mixed into the center or filling, the thickness of the chocolate shell, and the temperature and humidity at which the confection was stored.

SHELL-MOLDED TRUFFLE: See A Field Guide to Truffles, page 42.

SINGLE ORIGIN: See **Named origin**.

SUGAR BLOOM: A thin coating of sugar crystals on the surface of a piece of **chocolate**. Sugar bloom is the result of water condensing on the surface of a piece of chocolate, causing the sugar to seep out of the chocolate and crystallize on the surface. When this happens, not only is the visual appeal affected but the smooth and creamy texture of the chocolate is ruined. It is usually not possible to "fix" sugar-bloomed chocolate by melting and **tempering** it. However, you can often still bake with it.

TEMPER: Because **chocolate** does not contain water, it does not harden by evaporation. It hardens when the **cocoa butter** crystallizes. There are six different forms that the cocoa butter molecule can crystallize into, but only one of those six results in a chocolate with a crisp snap and a nice sheen. Tempering is the process of cooling melted chocolate in a controlled fashion to force the formation of desirable cocoa butter crystals.

TERROIR: *Terroir* is a French word that means "of the earth." A terroir **chocolate** is one that is made with beans that come from a particular plantation, region, or country; the name of the place where the beans were grown appears on the label. Terroir chocolates are usually called by another name: named origin, single origin, pure origin, or grand cru.

TONNE: A metric ton—1,000 kilograms, or about 2,200 pounds.

THEOBROMA CACAO: The Latin name for the **cacao** tree. Often abbreviated *T. cacao*. The word *theobroma* literally means "food of the gods."

TRANSFER: A technique used to decorate either shell-molded or enrobed **truffles**. Transfers are made by printing colored **cocoa butter** onto highly polished sheets of acetate. Multiple colors can be printed to form very intricate illustrations and designs. To apply a transfer to a shell-molded truffle, a special type of mold that holds a sheet of transfers is used. The transfer is inserted into the mold before **chocolate** is poured into it to create the shell. Transfers are applied to enrobed truffles after the centers have been coated with chocolate. In both cases, the warm chocolate melts the cocoa butter in the transfer, causing it to stick to the surface of the piece of chocolate. The polished surface of the acetate also imparts a highly desirable shine to the surface of the chocolate.

TRINITARIO: A hybrid of the **Criollo** and **Forastero** varieties of **cacao** developed on the island of Trinidad (hence the name) after a "blast" of unknown origin devastated most of the crop there. Trinitarios are considered to be a variety of fine flavor cacao.

TRUFFLE: The French word for a **chocolate** confection that is now applied to chocolates made using one of three major techniques: hand rolling, enrobing, and shell molding. Originally, the word *truffle* referred to a chocolate confection (now sometimes called a *truffe nature*, French for "natural truffle") with a roughly formed center made of **ganache** that was coated with cocoa powder and that resembled the truffle fungus, which is how it got its name. See A Field Guide to Truffles, page 42, for details.

UNIVERSAL: The name given to a machine that can be used to grind, **refine**, and **conche chocolate** because it performs all three of the major chocolate manufacturing steps. Universals can be quite small 110 pounds (50 kilograms) to more than a **tonne**.

VARIETAL: A varietal **chocolate** is one that is made from a specific type of bean, and the name of the bean appears on the label. Porcelana, for example, is the name of a particular variety of **Criollo** bean. Often, a place name is used to identify a varietal; for example, Ocumare 67. (The *67* refers to the breeder's control number. The first hybrid is numbered *1*, the second *2*, and so on.)

WHITE CHOCOLATE: True white chocolate is a confection containing **cocoa butter** but no cocoa solids (the powder, or brown stuff). Is white chocolate really and truly **chocolate**? Even the experts are divided on this one. Legally, according to the FDA, there is such a thing as white chocolate. Purists will say that because there are no cocoa solids in white chocolate it doesn't deserve to be called chocolate. In the end, no one can force you to eat anything you don't want to eat, so who cares what it's called and whether it's really chocolate or not?

WINNOW: Once the **cocoa bean** has been **roasted**, it needs to be separated from its shell. To do this, the roasted bean must first be cracked. This splits the meat of the cocoa bean (the **nib**) from the shell, which is also broken into bits. Because the shell fragments are lighter than the nib pieces, they can be separated using a combination of vibration and air blown past the vibrating beans.

INSIDE THE CHOCOPHILE.COM RATING SYSTEM

✳

Back in 1994 when I became interested in chocolate and set out to learn what I could, there were no widely used rating systems for chocolate to guide people in their purchasing decisions. Most of the rating systems in place then—and now, as a matter of fact—used a simple numerical scale, rating chocolate bars from 1 to 5 or 1 to 10. These are akin to the 50- or 100-point systems used to rate wines, and for nearly seven years I struggled to develop a rating system for chocolate that used a 100-point scale by assigning the various sensory characteristics of chocolate relative importance. Taste is most important, then comes texture. Smell should be next, but then what? And how much more important is taste than texture or texture than smell? As you can imagine, these were complicated and subjective decisions to make.

The great thing about a numerical scale is that it's easy to understand that a 95-rated chocolate is better than an 87-rated chocolate. The problem with this kind of rating scale, however, is that it doesn't take into account the vastly different types and styles of chocolate, which I strongly felt would be key to making my rating system more useful to chocolate lovers.

In the end, I created a system for rating chocolate that enables people to compare (metaphorically speaking) apples with apples and oranges with oranges, and that places its emphasis on value, or quality when compared with price. Ratings are a composite of the following four elements: style, price, type, and quality. For examples of my ratings of specific chocolates visit Chocophile.com.

STYLE

The chocolate under consideration will probably fall into one of the four major styles of chocolate making (discussed in more detail on page 43):

1. Belgian: lighter, sweeter, added flavors are distinct;
2. French: darker, more bitter, added flavors are subtle;
3. American: unsubtle overall, very sweet; or
4. Nouvelle American: less sweet, added flavors are clear and distinct but not overpowering.

PRICE

A major market research company divides the market for chocolate into the following four segments. Because many chocolate companies use these reports, I've adopted these price ranges:

1. Mass market: less than $15 per pound;
2. Mass-market premium: $15 to $25 per pound;
3. Gourmet: $25 to $40 per pound; and
4. Prestige: more than $40 per pound.

The price of a chocolate helps set expectations for quality, especially with respect to the ingredients that should be used.

- If you are buying chocolate in the "prestige" price range, you should expect nothing artificial as an ingredient, no non—cocoa butter fats in the chocolate, and especially no hydrogenated fats. These chocolates will have shelf lives measured in days or weeks. Virtually all chocolates in the prestige category will be handmade. You should also expect fastidious attention to detail in the fit and finish of the chocolates. Flavor profiles are likeliest to be in the French and nouvelle American styles.
- If you are buying chocolate in the "gourmet" price range, you can lower your expectations a little bit. You might find some no-no fats in the centers, but you should not expect any artificial colorings or

flavorings. The ingredients list will be a little longer and may include natural stabilizers and preservatives (such as sorbitol, a type of sugar). These chocolates will have shelf lives measured in weeks to months. Flavor profiles can be in any style but American, and will be well balanced but not as delicate as in prestige chocolates.

- If you are buying chocolates in the "mass-market premium" price range, you can lower your expectations a little more. You will most likely find some no-no fats in the chocolate, and there is a high likelihood that artificial flavorings will be used. Much production will be done by machine, and the flavor profiles will tend to be in the Belgian and American styles.
- When you are buying chocolates in the "mass market" price range, set your expectations even lower when it comes to ingredients and production techniques.

TYPE

Note the form the chocolate comes in and if it can be described by one of the follow modifiers.

Forms:

1. Bars;
2. Truffles;
3. Beverages;
4. Baked goods; or
5. Frozen.

Modifiers:

1. Organic;
2. Enhanced (so-called healthful or nutritional chocolate); or
3. Sugar-free.

QUALITY

The Chocophile.com rating system rates chocolate on seven different quality levels, set forth below from lowest to highest.

Bad: I would never willingly eat this chocolate again.

Poor: I can't find anything good to say about this chocolate.

Ordinary: This chocolate did not distinguish itself to me in any way.

Good: I found some things to like about this chocolate. I would eat it if it were given to me, and I might put it on my Favorites shelf, but only if there was room.

Very good: I liked a lot of things about this chocolate, and I would make room for it on my Favorites shelf. I would buy this chocolate to give as a gift.

Superior: I really liked *everything* about this chocolate. I would give it a place of honor on my Favorites shelf and share it with other chocophiles.

Extraordinary: It doesn't get any better than this. No, you *can't* have any of mine.

The quality ratings are the most subjective aspect of the rating system, but they make it possible to make meaningful comparisons about value, or the relationship between quality and price. The best-value chocolates are the ones with the highest quality rating in their price range, and often (for example), a superior gourmet chocolate that costs $35 per pound is a better value than a very good prestige chocolate that costs $45 per pound.

RESODURCES

✳

BOOKS

Here's a selection of fascinating books that contributed to my knowledge and understanding of chocolate—its history, character, social context, significance, and versatility. Many of these books are not directly about chocolate, but they do present information that makes it possible to look at chocolate as more than a delectable treat.

Most of these books are still in print and easily available through online or specialty booksellers. (Links to websites where you can easily purchase many of these books are provided at DiscoverChocolate.com.) Out-of-print books, can often be located through online services such as Alibris.com.

The True History of Chocolate, by Sophie and Michael Coe
Thames and Hudson, 1996
ISBN 0-500-01693-3

First published in 1996 and the first chocolate history book I read (in early 1998), *The True History of Chocolate* is the most complete book on the subject; it's the source for much of the history that is recounted in most chocolate books that have been published since. The sections dealing with the archaeology and anthropology of Mesoamerica are now out of date, as new findings shine light on the history and uses of cacao in pre-Columbian times. Despite this flaw, if you can read only one book on the history of chocolate this is the one to read.

1491, by Charles C. Mann
Knopf, 2005
ISBN 1-4000-4006-X

Although chocolate is barely mentioned in the book and does not appear as an index term, *1491* provides a fascinating look at new scholarship about the Americas prior to the arrival of Columbus. In particular, it provides insight into the ways the first inhabitants of the Americas changed the landscape to fit their needs and wants, and how adept they were as botanists developing entirely new foods (such as breeding modern maize, or corn, from teosinte). Although not directly discussed here, one implication is that pre-Mayans, as part of the domestication process of cacao, bred Criollo trees from Forastero trees.

The Botany of Desire: A Plant's-Eye View of the World, by Michael Pollan
Random House, 2002
ISBN 0-375-76039-3

The Botany of Desire looks at the relationships among humans and important domesticated plants: apples, tulips, marijuana, and potatoes. It challenged much of what I thought I knew about chocolate.

On Food and Cooking, by Harold McGee
Scribner, 2004
ISBN 0-684-80001-1

Originally written in 1984 and containing relatively little information about chocolate and cacao, the 2004 edition has been considerably expanded. *On Food and Cooking* is *the* essential reference if you want to understand the science of food, whether you are interested in making candy, baking bread, brewing, distilling, or simply cooking food. Less comprehensive but equally interesting is McGee's other book, *The Curious Cook*.

The Science of Chocolate, by Stephen T. Beckett
Royal Society of Chemistry, 2000
ISBN 0-85404-600-3

The Science of Chocolate provides a concise view of the chemical and physical properties of cacao and chocolate and the processes involved in making chocolate and certain types of candy. If Chapter 2 in this book, about how cacao becomes chocolate, made you interested in knowing more about the physics and chemistry behind roasting, grinding, dutching, refining, and conching, this is the next book to read on those subjects.

Fine Chocolates, Great Experience, by Jean-Pierre Wybauw
Callebaut, 2004
ISBN 90-209-5914-X

Jean-Pierre Wybauw is an acknowledged master in working with chocolate and is an accomplished speaker and teacher. Though I have already attended at least three seminars he has given, I never miss an opportunity to watch him work. *Fine Chocolates* is one of only two cookbooks that appear on this book list (the other is *The Essence of Chocolate*). It is for the serious chocolatier who not only wants to learn high-end chocolate-making techniques, but also wants to understand some of the chemistry and physics that make the recipes and techniques work so well. If you make candy or truffles for a living or it's a very serious hobby, you can't help but learn a lot from this book.

The New Taste of Chocolate: A Cultural and Natural History of Cacao with Recipes, by Maricel Presilla
Ten Speed Press, 2001
ISBN 1-58008-143-6

The New Taste of Chocolate presents a history of chocolate that focuses on the New World and especially Venezuela. A great deal of attention is paid to the challenges involved in propagating and growing cacao that is disease and pest resistant as well as tasty. One of the most interesting features of the book is a huge selection of photographs of all types of cacao pods that showcases the extremely wide varieties of colors and shapes that cacao pods can take, highlighting the difficulty of accurately identifying cacao varieties just by looking at surface characteristics (called phenotyping). This is one of the most beautiful of all the books on chocolate and rounds out an understanding of cacao in the Americas.

Crafting the Culture and History of French Chocolate, by Susan Terrio
University of California Press, 2000
ISBN 0-520-22126-5

This absorbing book delves deeply into French society's long relationship with chocolate, explaining not only its earliest history but also how artisan (craft) chocolatiers face up to stiff international competition that they helped to create. Most of the familiar names in French chocolate are mentioned at some point, along with many lesser-known but highly influential people and companies. I know of no comparable book for either Belgian or Swiss chocolate that would provide similar insights into their histories.

The Cambridge World History of Food, edited by Kenneth F. Kiple and Kriemhild Coneè Ornelas
Cambridge University Press, 2000
ISBN 0-521-40214-X

Spanning two volumes and more than two thousand pages, *The Cambridge World History of Food* is an encyclopedic reference book to pretty much everything humans eat. Although the current version was published before virtually all of the current research on cacao had been published, it is the breadth and depth of this book that makes it interesting.

The Lore of Spices: Their History, Nature, and Uses around the World, by J. O. Swahn
Nordbook, 1991
ISBN 1-57717-181-0

Spices played a key role in the drive to explore and colonize the parts of the world unknown to Europeans prior to the fifteenth century. This book delves into the uses and cultural history of more than forty spices. Beautiful botanical illustrations complement the text.

The International Cocoa Trade, by Robin Dand
John Wiley & Sons, 1997
ISBN 0-471-19055-1

This is the only book that provides a comprehensive look at the international business of cocoa as a commodity. It provides an informative discussion of the economics of planting cacao plantations, exhaustive detail on trade and contract rules for the various cocoa exchanges, and an in-depth review of quality assessment procedures. The author does not shy away from discussing issues of corruption that exist to this day. After reading this book you will marvel at just how complicated the cacao market is and understand a little better the hurdles that face startup chocolate-manufacturing companies that want to source beans directly.

The Essence of Chocolate: Recipes for Baking and Cooking with Fine Chocolate, by John Scharffenberger and Robert Steinberg
Hyperion, 2006
ISBN 1-4013-0283-6

In addition to the recipes, which range from mostly familiar uses of chocolate in desserts to more exotic savory preparations, the book includes stories of Scharffenberger's and Steinberg's personal experiences in the chocolate business. You'll enjoy some

lessons from experts about where cacao beans come from, what happens in plantations around the world, and how chocolate is made—all presented in an engaging back-and-forth interview-style format.

The Chocolate Connoisseur, by Chloé Doutre-Roussel
Tarcher, 2005
ISBN 1-58542-488-9

The Chocolate Connoisseur is an engaging historo-socio-technico-autobiography written by Chloé (there is only one Chloé in the chocolate world), who beat out 25,000 other applicants to become the head chocolate buyer for Fortnum and Mason, a leading upscale London department store, where for several years she helped influence the tastes of chocophiles around the world. Like me, Chloé is largely self-taught, so this book is a chronicle of her road to connoisseurship. Chloé has definite opinions about what constitutes bad and good chocolate; you may or may not agree with her, but she will get you to think more carefully about the chocolate you eat.

Chocolate: A Bittersweet Saga of Dark and Light, by Mort Rosenblum
North Point Press, 2005
ISBN 0-86547-635-7

Chocolate reads like a novel of personal discovery, but rather than focusing on the spiritual, the book focuses on author Mort Rosenblum's personal discovery of chocolate. Rosenblum's experience as a special correspondent for the Associated Press and as a former editor of the *International Herald Tribune* explains a great deal about the approachable tone and lively mix of subject matter, including personal reminiscences, scholarly research, and recipes.

Acknowledgments

To paraphrase William Shakespeare, "Some people are born to chocolate, some people achieve chocolate, and some people have chocolate thrust upon them."

Over the past dozen years it has been my pleasure and privilege to be involved with an exceptional group of people who, in addition to sharing my passion for chocolate, have encouraged me to continue my own journey of chocolate discovery. I certainly wasn't born into chocolate (I went to art school), and my own understanding and the recognition of my peers is something I have worked very hard to achieve over the course of more than a dozen years. Once I started to gain some notoriety, however, chocolate from all over the world began to be thrust upon me.

I would first like to thank the following chocolate manufacturers and their employees for their dedication and for their visions of what chocolate can be: Amedei, Barry-Callebaut, Bonnat (especially Stephane Bonnat, who welcomed a perfect stranger into his workshop and his home during the World Cup in 1998), Chocolove, Chocovic, Cluizel, Dagoba, Domori, El Rey, Felchlin (particularly Claude Schellenberger, for his patience and openness), Guittard (particularly Gary Guittard and Ed Seguine, for sharing their knowledge), Pralus, Scharffen Berger, Slitti, Valrhona, Venchi, and Vintage Chocolates (particularly Pierrick Chouard, for organizing the University of Chocolate, which I am very glad I attended twice). And here's to a new generation of artisan chocolate makers who are challenging perceptions of what good chocolate will be: Art Pollard of Amano Chocolates, Shawn Askinosie of Askinosie Chocolates, Steve DeVries of DeVries Chocolates, and Amy Singh, who at the age of ten or so first showed me that with determination and the ability to improvise it was possible to make really quite good chocolate in the home kitchen.

I would also like to thank the following chocolatiers who have graciously educated and supported my efforts in many different ways:
Fran and Dylan Bigelow/Fran's Chocolates; Jean-Francois Bonnet/Tumbador Chocolates; Richard Donnelley/Donnelley Chocolates; John, Joe, and Tara/Christopher Norman Chocolates; Jean-Paul Hévin; Robert Linxe/La Maison du Chocolat; Norman Love/Norman Love Confections; Fritz Knipschildt/Knipschildt Chocolatier; Jeff Sheppard/Lillie Belle Farms; Michael Recchiuti/Recchiuti Confections; Andrew Shotts/Garrison Confections; Bethany and Jesse Thouin/The Cocoa Tree; Kee Ling Tong/Kee's Chocolates; Jacques Torres/Chocolate Haven; Godiva.

There are many others who have helped me along the way, both professionally and personally:
Michael Schneider, Jeffrey Dryfoos, Matthew Stevens and the rest of the staff at Haymarket Group and Carymax; Maricel Presilla, Eric Case, John Kehoe, and Patricia Gadsby; and Professors Philippe Petite-Huegenin and Jean-Luc Battini and all my classmates at the Universities of Chocolate in 2003 and 2005.

Thanks also to Bill Shinker and Erin Moore at Gotham for believing in the concept right from the start and to everyone in sales, PR, and marketing at Gotham/Penguin for their work to make the project a success. And finally, thanks to Sharyn Rosart, Sarah Scheffel, and everyone else at Quirk Packaging for their hard work, creativity, and love of chocolate.

Index

Page numbers in *italics* indicate photographs with captions.

Photo Credits

AMANO ARTISAN CHOCOLATE: 55, 86 bottom (left)

© BRADY BRELINSKI: 2, 122 bottom

CHOCOLATERIE CLUIZEL: 42 bottom, 68

CHUAO CHOCOLATIER: 42, middle

DIGITAL CARTOGRAPHICS: 140–141, 142–143, 144

DREAMSTIME: © Pryzmat: 72; © Liv Friis-Larsen: 96

FOODPIX: © Imageshop: 6, 138; © Jan Oswald: 9; © Thinkstock Images: 12; © Penina: 16; © Leigh Beisch: 25; © Lisa Charles Watson: 32 middle; © Mary Ellen Bartley: 41; © Dennis Lane: 46; © Gary Moss: 62; © Paul Poplis: 90; © Charles Schiller: 114; © James Baigrie: 120; © Rachel Weill: 136

© CLAY GORDON: 54, 58, 66–67, 74 (except top right), 75, 86 top, 86 middle (left), 86 bottom (right), 87 top, 87 middle (both), 112

ISTOCKPHOTO: © Richard Waller: 19, 104 top; © Piotr Przeszlo: 21; © Ewa Brozek: 22; © Andreea Manciu: 26; © Phillip Jones: 32 top; © Kelly Brown: 32 bottom; © Sandra O'Claire: 39, 131; © Melissa King: 42 top; © Peter Finnie: 53; © Wojciech Krusinski: 60; © Ewen Cameron: 61; © Elena Korenbaum: 64; © John Sigler: 81; © Pali Rao: 85; © Alisha Shevlin: 87 bottom (right); © Tom Gufler: 104 bottom; © April Turner: 111; © Julie de Leseleuc: 113; © Christine Glade: 119; © Don Bayley: 122 top; © Torsten Schon: 125; © Alain Couillaud: 128; © Joshua Smith: 134

MAX FELCHLIN AG, CHOCOLATE MANUFACTURER, SWITZERLAND: © König & König: 86 middle (right); © König & König: 87 bottom (left)

STOCKFOOD: © Fresh Partners: 28; © Foodcollection: 37 top; © Uwe Bender: 37 middle; © Chris Alack: 37 bottom; © Food Image Source/William Brady: 48; © Martin Jacobs Photography: 78; © Jim Scherer Photography, Inc.: 83; © Brigette Sporrer: 89; © FabFoodPix: 93, 124; © Gerritt Buntrock: 100; © Richard Jung Photography: 133

TAVA: (www.tava.com.au): 74, top (right)